ASCENT TO NOTHINGNESS

ALEX KURIAN, CMI

Ascent to Nothingness

The Ascent to God according to John of the Cross

Edited by Andrew Tulloch

ST PAULS

Edited by Andrew Tulloch

The quotation from Farid al-din'Attar (opposite) was taken from F.C. Happold, *Mysticism: A Study and Anthology* (Middlesex, Penguin Books, 1970), 258.

The illustrations on pages 14 and 15 were taken from *The Collected Works of St John of the Cross* (Revised edition) (Fr K. Kavanaugh and O. Rodriguez) (Washington, DC: ICS Publications, 1991), 66, 67.

ST PAULS Publishing
Morpeth Terrace, London SW1P 1EP, U.K.
Moyglare Road, Maynooth, Co. Kildare, Ireland

ISBN 085439 591 1

Set by Tukan, High Wycombe
Produced in the EC
Printed by Interprint Limited, Marsa, Malta

ST PAULS is an activity of the priests and brothers
of the Society of St Paul who proclaim the Gospel
through the media of social communication

If thou dost desire to reach this abode of immortality, and to attain this exalted station, *divest thyself* first of Self, and then summon unto thyself a winged steed out of *nothingness*, to bear thee aloft. Clothe thyself with the garment of *nothingness*, and drink the cup of *annihilation*. Cover thy breast with a *nothingness*, and draw over thy head the robe of *nonexistence*. Set thy foot in the stirrup of complete *renunciation* and, looking straight before thee, ride the steed of *non-being* to the place where *nothing is*. Thou wilt be *lost* again and again, yet go on thy way in tranquillity, until at last thou shalt reach the world where thou are *lost altogether to Self.*"

Sufi mystic Farid al-din 'Attar

CONTENTS

ACKNOWLEDGEMENTS

This work is largely the fruit of co-operation and friendship. So it is with pleasure that I take the opportunity to acknowledge all those to whom I owe a debt of thanks. Among the innumerable gifts God has granted me all through these years of my earthly existence, it is the gift of friendship that I cherish most. In his marvellous care and concern for me, God has continually surrounded me with wonderful people; I have never felt a shortage of encouragement and support. The Rev Fr Jesús Castellano Cervera, the moderator of the doctoral thesis from which this book sprang, helped greatly with his open and generous approach. Any student who researches the life, writings and spirituality of John of the Cross will appreciate the benefit of having a scholar like Rev Fr Frederico Ruiz Salvador in his panel of moderators. Rev Fr Benedict Kanakappally, he too a moderator, provided the level of help and encouragement one would expect from an elder brother. With a heart brimming over with gratitude I thank the authorities and the staff of the Teresianum for the use of their facilities, and all the assistance they offered me while I was completing my doctoral studies.

Sr Dolores Wilson, MFIC, my fellow missionary in Papua New Guinea, spared her precious time to correct the language of the original thesis.

Here, too, I must thank Andrew Tulloch who, on behalf of St Pauls Publishing, took the utmost care to retain my ideas intact while performing the difficult task of reducing the length of my thesis in preparation for its publication, and doing further work on the language and presentation of ideas.

My brother CMIs and my friends enthusiastically

supported me during my research work through their critical comments and timely support. It will be a grave negligence on my part if I fail to mention some of them like Jacob Marangatt, Paulachan Kochappilly, Joy Kakkanatt, James Pampara, Augustine Thottakara, Lucas Vithuvattickal, et al.

I would like to express my special gratitude to Rev Fr Paul Kalluveettil, who has been a source of strength and inspiration in the vicissitudes of my life. How can I forget at this moment of happiness my parents, my uncle Rev Fr John Joseph CMI, members of my family, relatives, confreres, friends and my well-wishers for their prayerful support, encouragement and assistance. Finally, I wish to express sincere and profound gratitude to all the readers of this book.

Alex Kurian CMI

Abbreviations used in footnotes

1A	*Ascent of Mount Carmel*, book one
2A	*Ascent of Mount Carmel*, book two
3A	*Ascent of Mount Carmel*, book three
1N	*Night*, book one
2N	*Night*, book two
C	*Canticle*
LF	*Living Flame*
Prec	*Precautions*
Sayings	*Sayings of Light and Love*

Sketch of Mount Carmel by John of the Cross

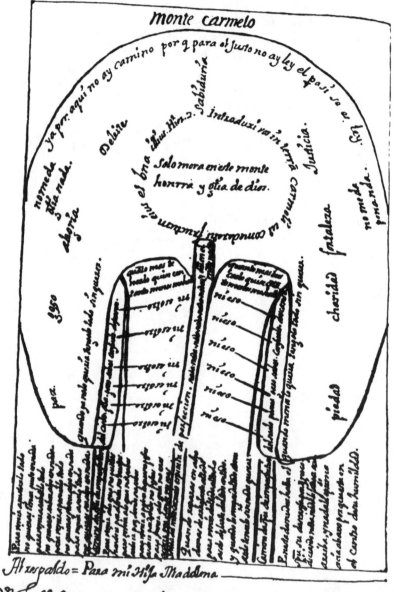

Sketch of Mount Carmel (English version)

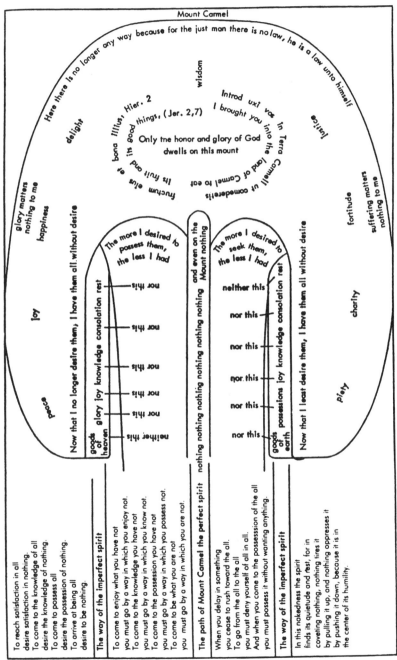

Mount Carmel

Here there is no longer any way because for the just man there is no law, he is a law unto himself

wisdom

delight

Introd uxi vos In Terra
bona Illius Hier . 2 I brought you into the
things, (Jer. 2,7) land of Carmel to eat

Only tne honor and glory of God
dwells on this mount

fructum elus et its fruit and
ut comederetis Its fruit

justice

glory matters nothing to me

happiness

Now that I no longer desire them, I have them all. without desire

suffering matters nothing to me

The more I desired to possess them, the less I had

and even on the Mount nothing

The more I desired to seek them, the less I had

joy

goods of heaven: glory joy knowledge consolation rest

nor this
nor this
nor this
nor this
neither this

nothing nothing nothing nothing nothing

neither this
nor this
nor this
nor. this
nor this
nor this

goods of earth: possessions joy knowledge consolation rest

fortitude

peace

The path of Mount Carmel the perfect spirit

Now that I least desire them, I have them all without desire

charity

piety

To reach satisfaction in all
desire satisfaction in nothing.
To come to the knowledge of all
desire the knowledge of nothing.
To come to possess all
desire the possession of nothing.
To arrive at being all
desire to be nothing.

The way of the imperfect spirit

To come to enjoy what you have not
you must go by a way in which you enjoy not.
To come to the knowledge you have not
you must go by a way in which you know not.
To come to the possession you have not
you must go by a way in which you possess not.
To come to be what you are not
you must go by a way in which you are not.

The path of Mount Carmel the perfect spirit

When you delay in something
you cease to rush toward the all.
To go from the all to the all
you must deny yourself of all in all.
And when you come to the possession of the all
you must possess it without wanting anything.

The way of the imperfect spirit

In this nakedness the spirit
finds its quietude and rest, for in
coveting nothing, nothing tires it
by pulling it up, and nothing oppresses it
by pushing it down, because it is in
the center of its humility.

Redesigned sketch of Mount Carmel

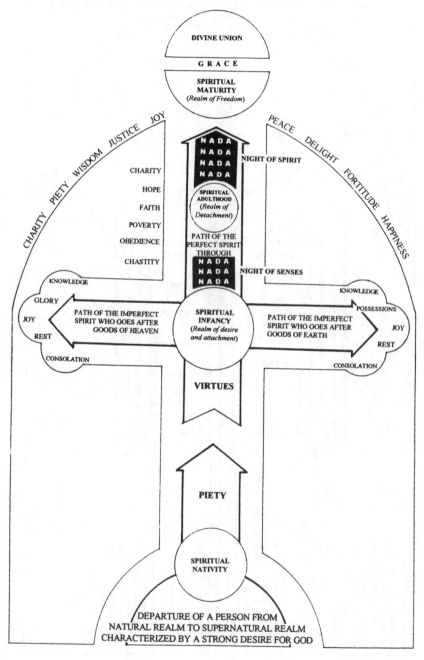

GENERAL INTRODUCTION

The works of John of the Cross do not compare in quantity or variety with the writings of other great Doctors of the Church. The focus of his doctrine remains always the same: union with God. Yet, in spirituality, especially in the field of mysticism, he has equals but no betters. His concept of *nada*[1] and its role in our reaching of *el todo*[2] has attracted the attention of spiritual seekers both from Christianity and from other religions. The reason for the universal acclaim awarded to John's spiritual writings could well be his straightforward, objective, heroic, disciplined, sober, factual, analytical and rational approach to his subject. John was never that sort of spiritual writer who with a gratuitous lack of restraint depicts heaven and hell to evoke the approved emotions in the reader. He never even attempted to tell us what heaven was like, but rather focused his energies on showing us how to walk the path of *nada* and live our life in perfect obedience to the Father here and now, with the absolute assurance of a blessed consummation.[3] The logic of his teachings is simple: God is all, and a soul that is already overcrowded cannot obtain a full measure of God's self-gift. For each person to possess God fully, according to their capacity, they should first empty themselves of everything else.[4] John's entire process of ascending *Mount Carmel* may be reduced to one maxim: from *nada* to *el todo*.

The principal problem in mystical theology is the non-communicability of the experience obtained through contact with God. One of the ways of dealing with this problem is the so-called *apophatic* or 'negative' (*apophatikos* meaning 'negative' in Greek) approach to God, which entails 'knowing by unknowing' and 'seeing by not seeing'. We will look a little more closely at this negative approach shortly, and again briefly in chapter one. Mysticism, understood as the 'practical' aspect of mystical theology, is, in its essence, an experience of God at the deepest centre of our being; it is a meeting with him. As such, the experience goes beyond the habitual conditioning of our senses and our emotional and intellectual responses, and brings about a gradual purification and a release from our given tendency to place ourselves at the centre of everything. This openness to God is attained gradually by means of an ever-intensifying reduction of our inordinate desires and the surrendering of our selves to his will. In this process of negation, the individual shatters, one after another, every chain that keeps them from experiencing perfect freedom. On this path to *el todo,* however, there are many quagmires. Anyone who dares to step on the path of *nada*, is taking the great risk of exposing themselves to the ferocious assaults of those forces of enslavement in human life that have traditionally been called the world, the flesh and the devil.

For those who take the path which leads to *el todo* by way of *nada*, John of the Cross is generally considered to be a safe guide, especially for beginners.[5] John warns us of the material as well as spiritual 'goods' on this path, which can become a trap if we are captivated by them. Even experienced persons run the risk of committing blunders in their 'discernment of spirits'. Proposing John as a guide in whom we can trust, Ruth Burrows says:

> John, it seems to me, has given us, as no one else, the absolutes of the spiritual life, the bedrock principles, the 'musts' deriving from who and what God is and what we are. His basic teachings... cannot be dismissed as one way among many. The power and authority of John lie precisely in that what he has laid bare for us are the *sine qua non* of it all, grounded on the reality of God and the reality of man... The core of John is nothing other than a stark presentation of the heart of the Gospel.[6]

John calls for freedom from all sorts of attachments except the one to God. He emphatically asserts that, "as soon as natural things are driven out of the enamoured soul, the divine things are naturally and supernaturally infused, since there can be no void in nature."[7] Here John is trying to tell us, "Empty your *ego*, and you will discover God's presence in the emptiness thus created." Since God is fullness, he can be present nowhere in his fullness except in emptiness. In other words, the God who is encountered in *nada* alone, is the real God and all of his other appearances are limited representations of him. Moreover, God transcends the human intellect, and is inaccessible to it.[8] Therefore, any God encountered by the human intellect is a limited God, who will soon turn into an idol and eclipse the real God, "who is a night to the soul in this life".[9] *Nada* is neither a disregard towards creation nor a depreciation of human potential: it is an openness to truth and a transcendent path to freedom.[10]

Nada has never been a best-seller in spirituality, especially among the followers of monotheistic religions. 'Nothingness' and the 'negative approach' have generally provoked more antagonism than appreciation. Very often Christian theologians, in their enquiries into the nature of our existence (the so-called 'metaphysical' questions) have given priority to the positive over the negative, to what is active over passive and to being over non-being. However, the egocentric misuse of nature and the environment by human beings, whose devastating effects threaten our planet and its future, has forced many thinkers to re-evaluate critically age-old beliefs, theories and practices. Not only science itself, but also philosophies and religions have been called into question on account of the ecological catastrophe that many see threatening our planet. The attitude of 'conquer and subdue' carried by monotheistic religions has been put forward as one of the reasons behind the over-exploitation of 'mother-nature' and the vandalism to which she has been subjected. On a more fundamental level, the concept of a transcendent God held by the monotheistic religions has often been criticised for its devaluation of creation, while oriental religions have been praised for their philosophy of the immanence of God and their eco-friendly lifestyle. The Buddhist wisdom on 'emptiness' attracted intellectuals and scientists to such an extent that it has been hailed as the only religious philosophy which can withstand the acid-test of time and human reason.[11] This challenged the rest of the world religions[12] to look to their own traditions for something similar. The interest in oriental wisdom and the increasing number of books written on this subject suggest that it is time to bring out the long-neglected treasures of Christianity.

To the credit of Christianity, it has had its own saints and mystics, like Gregory of Nyssa and a Syrian monk sometimes referred to as 'Pseudo-Dionysius', who, with a firm foundation in Scripture, proposed a way of 'unknowing' or 'negative way', which entails leaving behind the perceptions of the senses and the reasoning of the intellect, in order to reach the Ineffable.[13] A careful analysis of his writings proves that John was a worthy successor to these advocates of such a path. Being well-trained in the philosophy of his day and having a very sharp analytical mind, John provides us with a philosophical, theological and practical framework for the attainment of *el todo* through the practice of *nada*. John considered his 'Sketch of Mount Carmel' as the essence of his teachings[14] and therefore placed it at the beginning of his *Ascent* so that it could serve as a summary of the doctrine contained in this exposition. In the 'Sketch of Mount Carmel' we can see the synthesis of all his philosophical, theological and spiritual teachings. In fact, he made copies of this 'visual synthesis of his instructions' and distributed them among the nuns and friars of the Reformed Carmel who had been placed under his spiritual guidance. Unfortunately, John wrote no explanation of this important sketch, as had been the case with the commentaries he gave on his poems. The absence of such a document puts us at a disadvantage in our attempts to understand the *kenotic* (*kenosis*, a Greek term, means 'emptying') spirituality that evolves along his *nada* path. This difficulty notwithstanding, however, the 'Sketch of Mount Carmel' is central to this discussion of John's vision of *nada*, and the original sketch has been redesigned using John's own ideas gathered from his commentaries on his poems. This redesigning has been done in order to (hopefully) render more clearly and comprehensively John's vision of *nada*, tracing the *nada* path from its origin to its climax. An occasional reference to the 'Redesigned Sketch of Mount Carmel'[15] therefore will help the reader towards a clearer understanding of the subject matter.

As mentioned earlier, the Christian tradition has been too little engaged in the daunting challenge of exploring 'emptiness'. Even the beautiful hymn that Paul wrote to the Philippians (Phil 2:6-11) on the self-emptying of Christ was neglected for a less demanding view of the 'redeemer'. It may also be a surprise to observe that *nada*, a word which was repeated time and again in John's writings, has not been given enough serious attention by those who have been studying him and writing about him for the last four centuries. I hope to contribute to the present reassessment of this situation. The face of John which is revealed by this exploration may be surprising, but will hopefully prove itself to be quite Biblical, authentic and, above all, beneficial for the future of our world, and the planet on which we live.

My aim is to explore the way of *nada*. The following issues will also be considered: what exactly is the role of *kenosis* in the Christian spirituality? How can *kenosis* be lived in the Christian spiritual life? What is the scope of *kenotic* spirituality in the present and the future? In this exploration John himself is our guide, shedding light upon our path by means of his *nada* spirituality. The main sources are the writings of John themselves.[16] Quotations from other authors are mainly intended to give the reader a hint of how others look at those issues, though it does not necessarily imply agreement with them. This subject acquires additional relevance in the light of the encyclical letter *Fides et Ratio* of John Paul II, published in 1998, where the Pope pinpoints the "basic and urgent need" to analyse Scriptural and other traditional texts to understand the "grand and mysterious truth of *kenosis*". He says:

> From this vantage-point, the prime commitment of the theology is seen to be the understanding of God's *kenosis*, a grand and mysterious truth for the human mind, which finds it inconceivable that suffering and death can express a love which gives itself and seeks nothing in return. In this light, a careful analysis of texts emerges as a basic and urgent need: first the texts of Scripture, and then those which express the Church's living Tradition.[17]

This book is divided into four chapters. The first chapter, "*Nada* Spirituality of John of the Cross: Background and Foundations", analyses the various factors which might have contributed towards the development of John's *nada* spirituality. Here we briefly explore the political, social and cultural context into which John was born, consciously avoiding a detailed biographical sketch, because this has been done on many occasions elsewhere. John's biblical, patristic, philosophical and spiritual roots will be uncovered: we will thus be able to have a brief look at some of the great personalities in the field of Christian mysticism. The second chapter, "*Nada*: the Path of the Perfect Spirit" is a survey of the entire path of *nada* based on the 'Redesigned Sketch of Mount Carmel'. The *nada* path is divided into four stages, starting with spiritual birth and culminating in spiritual maturity. The two deviations that often occur on the path towards perfection, and their consequences are also illustrated in this chapter. The third chapter, "The Progressive Steps of *Nada*", concentrates on the practical aspects of John's '*nada*-path'. Here will be explained how growth in the traditional evangelical counsels and theological virtues is used to measure progress along the path of *nada*.

The fourth chapter, *"Aspects of Nada*: the 'Womb' of the 'Awakened Self'"*, deals with the effect of the *nada* experience in the life of an individual. This section helps us to understand *nada* from different angles. Jesus and Mary are presented as perfect examples of the *nada* life, the best role models available to humanity.

There are two areas of enormous potential that due to the constraints of space have to be left for future treatment, but are worth mentioning here. This book deals with the concept of 'nothingness' in the writings of John of the Cross, yet in the field of spirituality this concept has a long history. As mentioned earlier, in chapter one we will glance at a few of the Christian writers before John who have contributed to the development of this important concept. But we must also remember that the concept of nothingness has had a long history in Hinduism, Buddhism, Judaism and Islam, which lack of space will not allow us to explore. This is the first area we will have to leave aside. The second would be an exploration of the practical implications, challenges and hope John's *nada* spirituality offers the world of today. Particularly important are some of the predicaments humankind is faced with today, such as the ecological crisis or the need for religions to respond ever more effectively to the contemporary cries of the human heart.

All that aside, I hope that this book will offer the reader an insight into an absolutely central issue in religion and life, and that the following chapters will reveal the uniqueness and genius of the contribution made to this subject by the Spanish Carmelite, Juan de la Cruz.

NOTES

1 The Spanish word *nada* means 'nothing'.
2 The Spanish word *el todo* means 'the all'. John of the Cross holds the view that *'el todo'* [God] is reached through following the path of *nada* [nothing]. Cf. *1A* 13,11.

3 R. Burrows, *Ascent to Love: The Spiritual Teaching of St John of the Cross* (Bombay: St Paul Publications, 1990), 4.

4 L. of St Joseph, *The Secret of Sanctity of St John of the Cross* (tr., M. Alberto), (Milwaukee: The Bruce Publishing Company, 1962), 7.

5 R. Burrows, *Ascent to Love*, 4.

6 *Ibid.* 5.

7 *2A* 15,4.

8 *2A* 8,4.

9 *1A* 2,1.

10 R. Burrows, *Ascent to Love*, 7.

11 E. Benz, *Buddhism or Communism: Which holds the Future of Asia?* (London: George Allen & Unwin, 1966), 143-151; J. K. Locke, *Bihar: Land of the Buddha* (Patna: Navjyoti Prakashan, 1986), 29.

12 J.G. Arapura, "Buddhist Encounter with other World religions", *Journal of Dharma* 20/2 (1995), 109-110.

13 The 'negative way', or *via negativa* in Latin, is a theological method of denying God every possible attribute (even goodness). In the thought of Pseudo-Dionysius this method supersedes the 'positive way', the *via positiva*, which attributes to God all possible being and all 'perfections'. Many hold that the former method is more suited to the absolutely unknown nature of God. God can be known in two ways: by the intellect or by mystical contemplation. John's own affinity towards the path of negation and his repeated use of the word *nada* or 'nothingness' to describe the creation gave him the nickname 'Doctor of *nada*'.

In this context it is worth noting that Thomas Aquinas articulated a third way, what we would call the 'way of excellence', the *via eminentia*: any quality attributed to God, such as love, by way of *via positiva*, must be 'immersed' for a very long time in the 'bath' of the *via negativa* (not Thomas' expressions). The result of such an 'immersion' in this example is that, roughly, we realise that when God loves he loves in a way proportionate to infinite 'being', whereas we love in a way proportionate to our (limited) human nature. Thus for Thomas we can say true but inadequate things about God. (Thomas and Pseudo-Dionysius are not saying exactly the same thing.) John of the Cross appreciated this need to be able to say something about God, because if we can say nothing about God or *even just about the way he acts*, how can we say he loves us and so on?

After having got so far with knowledge, we now proceed in darkness, working by the way of love.

14 *1A* 13,10.

15 For the 'Redesigned Sketch of Mount Carmel' see page 16.

16 The translation used in this book is that of K. Kavanaugh and O. Rodriguez, *The Collected Works of St John of the Cross* (Revised Edition), (Washington, D.C.: ICS Publications,1991), amended where it seemed to me necessary.

17 P. John Paul II, *Fides et Ratio* (Encyclical letter), L'Osservatore Romano (Eng. ed.) N. 41 (1562), 14th Oct. 1998, n.93.

ONE

NADA SPIRITUALITY OF JOHN OF THE CROSS: BACKGROUND AND FOUNDATIONS

Much work has been done recently on John from a biographical, historical, literary and doctrinal point of view, with the result that we know more about him than ever before.[1] Many sources contributed to the formation of John's thought: they fused together in the blazing furnace of his personal experience to form his own unique spirituality. The writings that are left to us testify to the breadth and depth of this spirituality, as Allison Peers, the author of a classic biography on John and a translator of his works, testifies: "The writings of St John of the Cross form nothing less than a Contemplative library, and a library stacked with works of such profundity and fullness that few readers, even if trained for their task, could hope to assimilate it in a lifetime."[2] The range of these sources is wide: Thomas Aquinas and Scholastic theologians and philosophers in matters of structure, principles and ideas; Augustine and Neoplatonic philosophy for the constituent elements of the mystical life; the mystics of northern Europe for images, expressions, and experiences; Spanish mysticism for terms, problems, and language style; the poetry of his time for symbols, sensibility, and expressions; and Islam for his mystical attitudes.

The purpose of this chapter is to examine the background
and foundations of John's *nada* spirituality. The survey
begins with an overview of sixteenth century Spain, turning
then to consider how John encountered *nada* in his own
life, and what the term *nada* meant for him. It is clear,
however, that the reasons John had for choosing the path
of *nada* lie beyond the sum of his lived experiences. From
his study of the Scriptures he was convinced of the
transcendence of God and the futility of human attempts
to 'contain' him. A passage from the Scriptures which he
often quotes, "What no eye has seen, nor ear heard, nor the
human heart conceived, what God has prepared for those
who love him" (1 Cor 2:9; cf. Is 64:4),[3] forms the Scriptural
basis of his vision of *nada*. His only aim was to guide the
person to God, and since he knew the futility of every
human effort to attain that end, he turned to the Scriptures
for guidance. Having trawled that profound ocean of
wisdom, he discovered the concept of *nada*, the safest and
the shortest way to God. He announces the purpose of his
writings as follows:

> The discreet reader must always keep in mind my intention
> and goal in this book: to guide the soul in purity of faith
> through all its natural and supernatural apprehensions, in
> freedom from deception and every obstacle, to divine union
> with God.[4]

John's understanding of the Bible was thoroughly shaped
by the Scholastic theological and philosophical method of
the time in which he was trained. For this reason, as part of
our attempts to examine the theological foundations of
John's thought, it will be necessary to explore some of the
basic theological and psychological concepts of
Scholasticism. Furthermore, in search of the spiritual
foundations of John's works, we will briefly discuss a select
few of the great personages of the Patristic and Medieval
periods who might, directly or indirectly, have influenced
the development of his vision of *nada*.

Spain at the time of John

Spain in John's day was something of an 'India' of the West. It was a land of mysticism, and produced some of humanity's greatest mystics. Spain has a further claim to uniqueness: within her national boundaries arose mystics from the three great monotheistic religions of Christianity, Islam and Judaism. The great Ibn al-Arabi (1165-1240), whom many Sufis call 'the greatest sheikh', was from Murica. Moses de León, to whom *Zohar* – the masterpiece of Jewish mysticism – is attributed, was from Granada. León Hebreo, the author of the extraordinarily popular book *The dialogues of Love* (1535), was a Spanish Jew.

The middle of the fifteenth century saw the emergence of a multitude of native Spanish Christian writers. Though the majority of them were ascetics, there were among them real mystics as well. John of Avila (author of *The Book of Prayer*), Peter of Alcantara (*Treatise of Prayer and Meditation*), García Ximenes de Cisneros (*Exercises for the Spiritual Life*), Bernardino of Laredo (*The Ascent of Mount Sion*), Alonso de Orozco (*Mount of Contemplation*), Alonso of Madrid (*The Art of Serving God*), Ramon Lull (*Canticle of the Friend and the Beloved*) and Francisco de Osuna (*Third Spiritual Alphabet*), were all writing before John. These authors and their works were often mentioned by Teresa of Jesus (sometimes called Teresa of Avila) as guides in her spiritual formation, and were widely used by the Reformed Carmelites.

In political terms the sixteenth century was one of the most dynamic in the history of Spain, during which she achieved a greatness and glory never again equalled. In the seventh and eighth centuries Islam had eliminated more than half of Christendom. Encouraged by the Popes, Christendom struck back. The crusade in Spain itself resulted eventually in the reconquest of the entire Iberian Peninsula.

The marriage of Ferdinand of Aragon to Isabella of

Castille in 1469 consolidated a significant part of the Iberian Peninsula under a single dynasty. The union of Aragon in the east and Castille in the west was thus finally achieved, and the Trastámara became, after the Valois of France, the second most powerful monarch in Europe. The problems Ferdinand and Isabella had with their Moorish neighbours were primarily political and military and not religious. These Catholic Monarchs finally reconquered the Muslim Kingdom in a long and arduous campaign which ended with the capture of Granada, the capital, in 1492. The surrendering Muslims were initially offered generous terms, including religious freedom. A little later on, Francisco Jiménez de Cisneros, the Queen's confessor (later made Cardinal), introduced forced mass conversions against the advice of the saintly Hernando de Talavera, the archbishop of Granada, who was trying to convert the Muslims by precept and education. In 1502, the Muslims were offered the choice of baptism or exile. Many of them were baptised but continued to practise Islam secretly. In the same way the Muslims of Valencia and Aragon were baptised forcefully in 1526 and thereafter, Islam was officially banned in Spain.

The reconquest of Granada, the unification of the nation, and the riches brought from the New World colonies had a tremendous impact on the social, political and cultural life of the people. From a religious point of view, this was a troubled period. The Moorish problem, coupled with the general decadence of the Religious Orders and the clergy (in particular), led to the institution of the (Spanish) Inquisition by Ferdinand and Isabella. In response, the Religious Orders undertook to renew themselves, though with varying degrees of enthusiasm. Ultimately, this reform movement paved the way for a Catholic renaissance in Spain. John was born and brought up during this significant period of Spanish history.

Experience of *nada* in the life of John

Turning now to the details of John's own life, we will look at the bitter experiences he underwent that might have contributed towards the development of his spirituality of *nada*.[5] Three such specific periods of trials and tribulations of varying intensity stand out, all having a formative value. The fact is that the poverty that John suffered in the early years of his life, the misunderstandings and punishments he endured in the later years, the final persecution from his own brethren, might more easily have brought forth a bitter cynic; instead, the result was a man purified and enlightened.[6] His first encounter with *nada* was the effect of the biting realities of poverty he suffered as the child of a young widow; his second encounter with *nada* was the conflict the reform movement generated within the Carmelite Order, the response of the hierarchy being to single out John and orchestrate his arrest and imprisonment; the third and final encounter was more crucial and painful, as it was brought about by his own 'reformed brethren' and may well have contributed to his untimely death in his forties.

Initial encounter with *nada* as a poor child

John's father, Gonzalo de Yepes came from an influential and wealthy family; his mother Catalina Alvarez was a poor orphan girl who lived at the mercy of a widow from Fontiveros. The daring decision of Gonzalo to marry Catalina, despite the displeasure of his relatives, resulted in his being disowned and disinherited by the family. In spite of the initial difficulties they survived. Little Juan was born to them as their third son in the year 1542. The sickness and the untimely death of Gonzalo in 1545, after two years of suffering, was a great blow to the family. The penniless Catalina approached the relatives of Gonzalo for help, but her hope bore no fruit. The death of Luis, the second son, added further grief to the misery of the widow. With her two children Catalina moved to Medina del Campo, in the hope of improving their living conditions. There, at the age of nine, John started his schooling in an institution frequented mainly by orphans. He learned to serve the Mass, and as a result, Don Alonso Alvarez de Toledo, the administrator of the Hospital, noticed him and arranged for him a job in his hospital as a nurse.[7]

The encounter of the future John of the Cross with *nada* as a child was less severe than the later encounters for three reasons. Firstly, he had a loving and protective mother to take care of him. Secondly, poverty, although fatiguing and humiliating, was not a personal deficiency; little Juan was merely a silent victim of an unjust society. Thirdly, the bodily suffering caused by poverty is not as acute as mental agonies arising from more subtle causes. The experience of poverty, moreover, has certain benefits and advantages of its own: poverty helps a person to get in touch with the realities of human life; it makes life simple; God and prayer become necessities rather than obligations; it creates a sense of dependence, not only on God, but also on others, thus enabling warm relationships to develop. Poverty creates an awareness of the needs of others and thus generates a compassionate and generous heart. Above all, poverty may contribute towards the development of an extraordinarily strong personality that can withstand trials, tribulations and even humiliations.

Second encounter with *nada* as a rebellious religious

The meeting with Teresa of Jesus in 1567 was a turning point in John's life. He worked with her in her attempts to reform the Carmelite Order. The tension between the 'Traditionalists' and the 'Reformers' grew stronger. John, being a founding member of the reformed Carmel, became the symbol of the reform movement and was arrested on the night of 2 December 1577 by a group of Carmelite friars and armed guards from the hermitage near the convent of the Incarnation at Avila. His days of imprisonment were severe and involved bodily as well as mental torture. Due to the long and rigorous imprisonment, his body was on the verge of collapse, but his spirit had grown stronger and was ready to begin a new phase in his life. After nine months of imprisonment, he came out of that 'womb of *nada*', 'one dark night', to sing to the world a new canticle of spiritual enlightenment.[8]

John's second encounter with *nada* was harsher than the former one, not only because it consisted of both physical and mental suffering, but also for three specific reasons. Firstly, he was directly accused of breaching the law. As a devout religious this was a source of great grief for him. He was even depicted as a rebellious religious, which meant that he had to defend himself. Secondly, he was portrayed as a person who was trying to destroy Carmel while, in reality, his aim was to enable her to be truer to her aims. Thirdly, he was isolated from all his supporters to such an extent that a complete mental breakdown was not impossible. He often heard reports of the total collapse of the reform movement and of its total failure. He was asked to abandon his 'hostile' attitude towards his Order and was tempted with some profitable and promising positions within it.

This second encounter with *nada* had its benefits, too. First and foremost, it gave him an opportunity to have a first-hand experience of the trials and tribulations of *nada*. It also gave him a chance to evaluate and reconsider his stance, and to reaffirm his own choices. The loss of contact with his supporters enabled him to enter into more intimate contact with God. He discovered through his own personal experience that God is the best comforter of the afflicted. His decisive rejection of the offers made by his captors, who promised both freedom and personal advancement, reaffirmed his commitment to his ideals and enabled him to grow in the virtue of hope. The physical torture that was inflicted upon him during the period of his imprisonment helped him to grow in humility and patient suffering. The isolated life of nine months in captivity opened his eyes towards the beauty of nature.

Final encounter with *nada* as an unwanted religious

John's final encounter with *nada* was much more acute and painful than both of his earlier two encounters because this last assault came from an unexpected source: his own brethren. In the year 1582 Teresa died. In 1585 Nicholas Doria was elected as the new provincial, and took upon himself the responsibility of renewing the troubled order of Teresa according to his own whims and fancies. Doria was displeased with John's position regarding the development of Teresa's reforms, and decided to get rid of him by sending him to Mexico. However, due to John's failing health, the decision was revoked and he was sent to la Peñuela instead. With Doria's knowledge, a friar began a campaign to discredit John and have him expelled from the Order. By 12 September 1591 John became seriously ill and was sent to Ubeda for treatment, where he received a very cold welcome. After three months of increasing illness John of the Cross died on 14 December 1591.

As mentioned earlier, John's last encounter with *nada* was his peak experience of *kenosis*, bearing a resemblance to that of Jesus. Jesus was rejected by his own disciples. His own people cried: "Crucify him!" (Lk 23:20). The last resort of Jesus was his heavenly Father, who also seemingly turned his face away from his Son, when his assurance was most needed. In the physical and mental torture that John endured during his days of imprisonment, he had the consolation that his persecutors were the opponents of the reform movement and not his personal enemies. Moreover, his oppressors were not questioning his personal integrity. They tortured him not because of his personal sins but because of his ideas. As a founding member of the reform movement, his victimisation was quite obvious and natural. They punished him because he was the symbol of the reform movement. Here, then, was an honourable cause for John to uphold as the reason of his humiliation and suffering. But in this third trial all the accusations against him were personal. It was the integrity of his character, and not his ideals, which was under attack. His own successors were his pursuers, who wanted to discredit him and to expel him from the reformed Carmelite Order, the very Order for which he had undergone lifelong suffering and even imprisonment. The physical torture inflicted upon a person by their opponents often attracts sympathy and support, or at least gives the victim a chance to feel pity for their own plight. The physical pain which John endured during the last phase of his life was not caused by any of his enemies but was the result of his own ailing body. The mental pain which he endured at this final stage was inflicted not by outsiders, but by the members of his own Reformed Carmel. Thus, he came face to face with *nada* as an unwanted, sickly religious whose personal integrity was dubious and under attack. He decided to surrender silently and meekly, but with a profound serenity, following the example of his role model – Jesus of Nazareth. When the clock struck midnight (14 December 1591) and the monastery bell tolled for Matins, he surrendered his 'self' to *nada*, irrevocably, and for the last time.

The meaning of *nada* in John's works

The word *nada* has its origin in a form of the Spanish verb *nacer* which means 'to be born'. Originally the word *nada* meant *cosa nacida* (something born), that is, something that exists. In order to describe a state of 'non-existence' the prefix *no* was added to the word *nada,* thus changing it to *nonada,* that is, not born, no-thing or non-existent. Gradually the prefix *no* was suppressed from *nonada* without any change in its meaning. Thus, the word *nada* now meant, nothing, nothingness, emptiness, non-existence, and so on.[9] John used the word *nada* in a variety of ways and with different levels of meaning, principally metaphorical, psychological and philosophical. On the whole, John had more affinity with its philosophical meaning than with the others. Whatever the case, the first thing to note regarding John's concept of *nada* is the primary place it occupied in his thoughts and writings. At the very outset, too, we would do well to notice that John's concept of *nada* was not atheistic. For him, *nada* is the way to *el todo.* Without *el todo* the path of *nada* makes no sense for him; it is in order to reach *el todo* that John suggests the path of *nada.*

John maintains that by nature we are *nada,* and the entire creation is *nada.*[10] We are called to realise this 'nothingness' that we are. This realisation will, ultimately, lead us to *el todo.* When we and our world dissipate into *nada,* the 'unfathomable nothingness', what remains is *el todo,* the 'uncreated existence'. In *nada* dissolves the 'insatiable possessor', the 'ego-self', and the person is made worthy of receiving the incoming God. In a person who has realised *nada,* there is no more 'ego' to 'possess' the incoming God. God simply 'enters' the heart of that person, which remains wounded due to the absence of the divine 'lover'. This means that those who interpret 'union' as the summit of John's mount, are not exactly following his thought. The summit of the mount is *nada,* and it is a place "where no one appeared".[11] At the top of the *nada*-path, right at the centre of the 'Sketch of Mount Carmel', John of the Cross wrote, "even on the mount is *nada*". To make his position very clear, he wrote again, "only the honour and glory of God dwell on this mount". This means that on the mount there are no 'rooms' for self-seeking 'egos' who, out of their insatiable greed for pleasure and possession, want to acquire God, the most coveted amongst the trophies. On the mount, besides "the honour and glory of God", there abides only *nada*. Whoever enters *nada* abides on the mount.

It is equally fundamental for John that it is 'humanly' impossible to achieve union with God. The path of *nada* that he proposed was not intended to terminate in union with God, but "to reach the nakedness of spirit".[12] Union with God is a gratuitous gift on the part of God, which he may or may not bestow: there are quite a few 'fortunate ones' who, by the grace of God, receive that 'out-of-the-world-experience' during their lifetime. It is, precisely, because of the gratuitousness of God's gift that the bride in *Living Flame* with great trust and hope implores God, "now consummate! if it be your will".[13] This and similar pleadings clearly prove that the aim of the ascent is to arrive at 'nothing'. Union is not the goal but a possible consequence of one's ascent to 'nothingness'. It is for God to decide whether the experience of union be granted to a particular person who waits for him. In his commentary on *Spiritual Canticle,* John explains this more clearly:

> this is a characteristic of the union of the soul with God in spiritual marriage: God works in and communicates Himself to her through Himself alone, without using as means the angels or natural ability, for exterior and interior senses, and all creatures, and even the soul herself does very little toward the reception of the remarkable supernatural favours that God grants in this state. These favours do not fall within the province of the soul's natural ability or work or diligence, but God alone grants them to her.[14]

Even so-called 'human effort' itself is understood by John as "sheer grace".[15] God's initiative and constant support is required to progress on the path of *nada*. However, John does hold the opinion that when the person co-operates with God's grace and practises self-knowledge and self-negation, a visit from 'above' is not far away. *Nada* is the thirst of a flaming heart "fired with the urgent longings of love"[16] to accommodate the beloved by emptying itself of the self. John's spirituality of *nada* is essentially love-generated and love-oriented. His expression 'all is nothing', as well as his emphasis on self-denial, mortification, emptiness, renunciation, nakedness, contempt for self and creatures, detachment, and so on, seem frightening only when they are taken out of context. The *Canticle*, if nothing else, shows that John was a lover of nature and recognised the true value of creatures; his love for Francisco his older brother reveals the value he set on friendship: "This is my brother – the greatest treasure I have in the world!", he is reported to have said on more than one occasion.[17] John calls creatures *nada* only in comparison with God. He opposes them only when they are placed on the throne of God. For the human heart is the abode of God. Creatures should not occupy God's seat: the human heart should remain empty and free for God.

At times John used the term *nada* as a last resort to explain some of his very intimate experiences and ideas regarding the ineffable mysteries of God. From the point of view of experience, '*nada* consciousness' means to have the taste of the void or to have experienced emptiness, that is, to encounter 'nothingness'. This experience approaches the reality of God more truly than any other because it touches him as he is, beyond feelings, images and concepts:[18] "Although at times individuals use words in reference to this knowledge, they clearly realise that they have said nothing of what they experienced, for no term can give adequate expression to it."[19] John often makes use of images like "place you know not",[20] "dark water",[21] "unbounded desert",[22] "dark belly of the whale",[23] "sepulchre of dark death",[24] "mid-air",[25] "deepest centre",[26] "secret abyss",[27] and so on, in order to explain this 'experience of nothingness'.

John used the term *nada* constantly not only because of the ineffectiveness of the human language to convey his inexplicable experiences, but also because he wanted to say something about God, in particular 'where' he acts. Human faculties for all their usefulness cannot help us to enter dimensions which are beyond their ken. The faculties must be left behind, therefore, if we are to acquire the nakedness of spirit which is necessary to enter the spiritual realm where God dwells. As mentioned earlier, *nada* is the "place where no one appears";[28] the four stanzas that follow this line from the poem 'Dark Night' indicate the location where the union between the soul and her beloved is consummated – it is the 'place of nothingness'. Because this place of nothingness is unfamiliar territory, the human mind cannot fully comprehend the incomparable experience that takes place there:

> Besides its usual effect, this mystical wisdom occasionally so engulfs souls in its secret abyss that they have the keen awareness of being brought into a place far removed from every creature. They accordingly feel that they have been led into a remarkably deep and vast wilderness unattainable by any human creature, into an immense, unbounded desert, the more delightful, savorous, and loving, the deeper, vaster, and more solitary it is. They are conscious of being so much more hidden, the more they are elevated above every temporal creature[29]... What God communicates to the soul in this intimate union is totally beyond words. One can say nothing about it, just as one can say nothing about God himself that resembles him. For in the transformation of the soul in God, it is God who communicates himself with admirable glory; the two become one.[30]

Biblical foundations of *nada*

The basis of John's spiritual synthesis is the Bible. His writings are packed full of biblical quotations and allusions from beginning to end. The passion and death of Jesus constitutes the backbone of his spirituality and thought:

the cross of Christ emerges as the ultimate experience of nothingness and consequently as the definitive proof of the central place of *nada* in his mystical theology. In John's vision, the doctrine of *nada* is derived from the central message of the Bible.

Old Testament understanding of *nada*

There are approximately 1,500 quotations from the Bible in John's writings, about two thirds of which are from the Old Testament.[31] He quotes mostly from the Pentateuch, the historical books, prophets, and the wisdom literature. Through the events recorded in the Old Testament John sees the Spirit speaking to present-day situations. Idolatrous Israel provides John with explanations of the appetites in his first book of the *Ascent of Mount Carmel*; Job, the Psalmist, and Jeremiah serve to explain the suffering in the second night of the spirit; and the *Song of Songs* serves to explain the state of union of love.[32] John identifies himself with some of the Old Testament personalities like Moses, David, the Psalmist, Job, and Jeremiah, who exemplify certain concrete, personal experiences. The disciplining undergone by the people of Israel in the desert was seen by John as an example for the new Israel of Christian believers on its path towards the new promised land. On the mount of perfection, like Mount Sinai of old, the 'beasts of appetites' are forbidden to wander, and undistracted attention to God is to be developed through the total annihilation of the 'beasts of desire'. This pilgrimage to the heavenly Jerusalem is not only a collective endeavour, but has its personal obligations too. The pilgrimage does not consist in the accumulation of virtues, but the denuding of the person of the possessions they covet, in order to prepare them for union with God. John names this denudation of everything other than God, the 'perfect virtue':

those who ascend this mount of perfection to converse with God must not only renounce all things by leaving them at the bottom, but also restrict their appetites (the beasts) from pasturing on the mountainside, on things that are not purely God. For in God, or in the state of perfection, all appetites cease. The road and ascent to God, then, necessarily demand a habitual effort to renounce and mortify the appetites; the sooner this mortification is achieved, the sooner the soul reaches the top. But until the appetites are eliminated, one will not arrive no matter how much virtue is practised. For one will be failing to acquire perfect virtue, which lies in keeping the soul empty, naked, and purified of every appetite.[33]

In order to be united with the transcendent God, one has to transcend everything that is not God.[34] In proof of this, John points to the first commandment. He spends the entire fifth chapter of the first book of *Ascent* proving the necessity of considering everything other than God as *nada*; this he does by citing various aspects of the first commandment. For John, this commandment that forbids the following of false Gods becomes the basis of the two nights. By citing Deuteronomy 6:5, John speaks of another aspect of this same commandment, an aspect which derives from love. In this verse, Moses beseeches the Israelites to love the Lord with all their heart, all their soul and all their might. The sole motivation for a person's relentless quest for nothingness is total and undivided love for God. The *nada* to *el todo* motif steers John's whole process of 'ascent'.

The first commandment points also to the 'nothingness' of all the forces of nature operating on the face of the earth. Every inordinate appetite, however small, is potentially an idol. To offer God a seat along with numerous other idols is sacrilegious as well as outrageous.[35] Before the omnipotent Yahweh all the false gods and their powers are *nada*. All those who worship anything other than God, will perish along with the idols they worship (cf. 1 Sam 5:2-4; Ps 113:8; Gen 35:2; Lev 26:1). John, like the prophets of the Old Testament, felt himself impelled to proclaim the living God and to show that there are no other gods like God, and that the only way towards him is the path of *nada*. In insisting on this he is like Elijah, who destroyed Jezbel's idols and journeyed to Mount Horeb, where he encountered the living God (1 Kgs 18:19). By citing the adventures of prophet Elijah (1 Kgs 18:20-45), John illustrates how displeasing idolatry is to God. In the first book of *Ascent* John quotes from the prophet Jeremiah to explain the two evil things the people of Israel had committed. They abandoned God, the source of living water and dug pits that held no water (Jer 2:13). The transcendence of all things through the application of *nada* is the wish and command of God. John teaches that the practice of the theological virtue of charity and the fulfilment of the first commandment of God necessitates a person to walk on the path of *nada*. He explains:

> This passage contains all that spiritual persons must do and all I must teach them here if they are to reach God by union of the will through charity. In it human beings receive the command to employ all the faculties, appetites, operations, and emotions of their soul in God so that they will use all this ability and strength for nothing else, in accord with David's words: *Fortitudinem meam ad te custodiam* (I will keep my strength for you) (Ps 58:10).[36]

From this perspective, it becomes apparent that John's seemingly nihilistic maxims are just practical applications and explanations of the first commandment. John was never against anything beautiful or enjoyable. He was not, in fact, against possession, knowledge or pleasure. John opposed only that kind of attachment and desire that withheld the person from advancing further towards their ultimate goal. For him the culmination of the spiritual ascent is *el todo* – the fullness of every possible good. Any 'part' that withholds the person from the 'whole', whether material or spiritual, natural or supernatural, was opposed by him.

Gospel teaching on *nada*

Jesus' radical statement concerning discipleship, "So therefore, none of you can become my disciple if you do not give up all your possessions" (Lk 14:33), was a favourite text of John's and we find it repeated four times in his writings.[37] The idea of renunciation implicit in John's writings is very precise and clear: give up all that is not God. The person must get rid of all appetites for natural and supernatural things that can otherwise be a hindrance to the union with God.[38] This means that no creature can be regarded as a greater, or lesser, impediment than any other. Any attachment to anything is a hindrance, since it may hold us back from God. Pure negation of everything is the perfect way.[39] In the third book of *Ascent*[40], John lists all the goods that should be abandoned, by not investing our expectations of joy in them, on the way to God; his list begins with material riches and ends with the divine revelations. In John's understanding, renouncing is a mental rather than a physical activity. Renouncing means "withdrawing the affection for"[41] or emptying the "great attachment"[42] towards goods, since God is the only good that can satisfy the human quest.[43] Jesus affirms that the love of God is the first and the greatest of all commandments (Mt 22:37), which has to be demonstrated by means of uncompromising obedience. The cross was, for Jesus, the fulfilment and high point of both his mission and his life of faithfulness to the Father's will (Mt 26:42). The Gospels portray Jesus as having clear presentiments of his life and mission culminating on the cross (Mt 8:13; 16:21; Lk 9:22). His lifelong obedience finds its perfection in his final option for a violent death.[44] So profound was his awareness of the benefits of the cross that for those whom he summoned to follow him, he made the readiness to take it up mandatory. We find the following demand of Jesus reiterated five times in the synoptics: "If any want to become my followers, let them deny themselves and take up their cross and follow me" (Mt 16:24; cf. also Mk 8:31; Mt 10:38; Lk 9:23; 14:27). Discipleship demands renunciation of family, occupation, possessions, and social standing (Mk 10:29-30).

Jesus forsaken

Jesus is the most compelling example of abandonment to God's will. His life was a constant search for his Father's will and pleasure; at the end of it, he entered the deepest possible openness to God through his passion, death, and resurrection. Jesus' most profound communion with God took place in his death and resurrection.[45] Surprisingly, perhaps, the Gospels reveal that Jesus did not himself fully understand this process of abandonment and that it caused him terrible suffering (cf. for instance Mt 26:39; Mk 15:34). Likewise, a spiritual person never understands fully what happens to them in their encounter with 'nothingness'. This incomprehension is an essential element in the experience of *nada*. The experience of losing oneself to nothingness is clearly demonstrated by Jesus on the cross when he cried out, "My God, my God, why have you forsaken me?" (Mt 27:46; Mk 15:34).[46] Jesus, who plunged into suffering and was forsaken by his Father, is the perfect model of abandonment, for he was brought to nothingness in his death on the cross. An imitation of Christ means total abandonment of the self. When the person is reduced to nothingness, spiritual union between them and God is effected, which is the greatest and highest state attainable in this life. In this process individuals suffer considerable affliction since they do not find any support or satisfaction. They come to believe that there would be no more spiritual blessings for them and that God has abandoned them.[47]

According to John, Jesus underwent the 'dark night of the senses and of the spirit', which signals the entrance into the absolute, more profoundly than any other mystic of the negative tradition. John refers to Matthew 27:46, "And about three o'clock Jesus cried with a loud voice, 'Eli, Eli, lema sabachthani?' that is, 'My God, my God, why have you forsaken me?'", and concludes that at this time of extreme abandonment, Jesus joined his Father to the fullest extent and his will became his Father's will. In the terrible ruin on the cross, the dying Christ experienced not only the abandonment of the world, but also the abandonment of his God.[48]

The highest degree of union is achieved when the person is reduced to nothing and humbled to the most extreme degree. The transition from the old to the new is not easy. Neither the loss nor the recovery of God's closeness happens in a flash. The old often disappears before the new is in sight. There often occurs a long blank period when nothing seems to be happening. Although this transition is unpleasant, it is necessary to further grow in intimacy with God. The contemplative must let the past die in order to enjoy a deeper relationship in the future. John explains this process as follows:

> and that they might realize that their union with God and the greatness of the work they accomplish will be measured by their annihilation of themselves for God in the sensory and spiritual parts of their souls. When they are reduced to nothing, the highest degree of humility, the spiritual union between their souls and God will be an accomplished fact.[49]

That they may be one as we are one

For John, we were created for love.[50] The purpose or the end of our being is the union of love.[51] The rigorous path a person has to tread, especially in the initial stages, is a preparation for the forthcoming feast of love. Passing through the preparatory stages, the person reaches the state of perfection, which is union with God.[52] This state is nothing but the taking part in the divine nature (2 Pt 1:4).

As a result of renunciation, the person undergoes a transformation and becomes a child of God. This process of transition was taught and accomplished by Jesus himself. Union with God, "the most noble and sublime state attainable in this life",[53] is modelled on the example set by Jesus Christ. Therefore, this sharing in God's nature is nothing but 'Christification' which is to be attained through the crucifixion of the ego. The end of the journey is thus union with the Word incarnate.[54] As Pope John Paul II states in his encyclical *Fides et Ratio* quoting from *Dei Verbum* (the Dogmatic Constitution on Divine Revelation of Vatican II), "After speaking in many places and varied ways through the prophets, God 'last of all in these days has spoken to us by his Son' (Heb 1:1-2). For he sent his Son, the eternal Word who enlightens all people, so that he might dwell among them and tell them the innermost realities about God (cf. Jn 1:1-18)."[55] The journey of Jesus, the head of the mystical body, *from* his Father *to* his Father, entirely following the path of *kenosis*, is the pattern for the 'rest of his mystical body' in its pursuit of its destination. In *Canticle* John clarifies this further:

> No knowledge or power can describe how this happens, unless by explaining how the Son of God attained and merited such a high state for us *the power to be children of God*, as St John says (Jn 1:12). Thus the Son asked of the Father in St John's Gospel: *Father, I desire that where I am those you have given me may also be with me, that they may see the glory you have given me* (Jn 17:24), that is, that they may perform in us by participation the same work that I do by nature; that is, breathe the Holy Spirit. And he adds: *I do not ask, Father, only for those present, but for those also who will believe in me through their doctrine; that all of them may be one as you, Father, in me and I in you, that thus they be one in us. The glory which you have given me I have given them that may be one as we are one, I in them and you in me; that they may be perfect in one; that the world may know that you have sent me and loved them as you have loved me* (Jn 17:20-23). The Father loves them by communicating to them the same love he communicates to the Son, though not naturally as

to the Son but, as we said, through unity and transformation of love. It should not be thought that the Son desires here to ask the Father that the saints be one with him essentially and naturally as the Son is with the Father, but that they may be so through the union of love, just as the Father and the Son are one in unity of love.[56]

The union which the evangelist and John envisage here is beyond the Old Testament correlative relationship – of opposite and counterpart – between Yahweh and Israel.[57] To the degree that the person conforms their entire life – sense and spirit – to the self-emptying of Jesus Christ in response to the will of the Father, they are led interiorly by the Spirit of God. Full conformity with the will of the Father is the essence of the adoption of the children of God:

> This is the adoption of the children of God, who will indeed declare to God what the Son said to the Eternal Father through St John: *All my things are yours, and yours mine* (Jn 17:10). He says this by essence, since he is the natural Son of God, and we say it by participation, since we are adopted children. He declared this not only for himself, the Head, but for his whole mystical body, the Church, which on the day of their triumph, when she sees God face to face, will participate in the very beauty of the Bridegroom.[58]

Deification and contemplation

Using biblical ideals, like humanity's partaking in the divine nature (2 Pt 1:4) and its becoming children of God (Gal 4:5ff), Christian tradition developed the concept of 'deification' or 'divinisation'. This concept, seen by some as an alien import into Christianity from the surrounding Hellenistic culture, actually has a solid biblical foundation, if we know how to use the Scriptural evidence without forcing it (see also, for instance, Gen 1:26f; Mt 5:41-48; Jn 3:1-3). It was used by the Fathers of the Church, whose influence on John we will consider later in the chapter, to express the newness of the condition to which humankind has been restored through the Incarnation of the Son of God. John used it to explain how God's action works on the human person, and the union of love to which we are called. In the Scriptures, too, John found authorisation for the emphasis of Greek thought on the vision or contemplation (theoria) of God as the goal of human blessedness: "Blessed are the pure in heart, for they will see God" (Mt 5:8).

Paul's vision of Jesus as 'God in *kenosis*'

Edith Stein, the Carmelite nun and Jewess who died in Hitler's gas chamber, saw in the letters of Paul a fully formed science of the cross.[59] Paul presents in his letter to the Philippians a Christ who 'emptied' himself and "became obedient to the point of death – even death on a cross" (Phil 2:8). Paul's intimate experience of *nada* on his way to Damascus (Acts 9:3-9) also might have helped him to develop this idea of *kenosis*. The 'self-emptying' of Jesus, according to Paul, is related to 'non-clinging' (cf. Phil 2:6-8ff). Jesus neither clung to the divine, nor to the profane, but preferred 'emptiness'. Jesus was willing to empty himself of all that was special and lived a life of faith, travelling through the night of unknowing. Eventually, he came to the ultimate night, the darkness of the cross, where his obedience brought him to the deepest sense of desolation.[60] His *kenosis* was so total that he lost contact with his Father. Just as he willingly abandoned his divine life in his incarnation, he willingly abandoned his human life on the cross. He is therefore the perfect model of total self-emptying. Paul modelled his life according to the pattern of the self-emptying of Christ. Jesus "humbled himself and became obedient to the point of death" (Phil 2:8). Paul found his glory in the cross of Jesus Christ, by whom the world was crucified to him and he to the world (Gal 6:14). Paul considered the humanity of Christ important since it is his humanity that shows us how to empty ourselves. The essence of the humanity of Jesus is self-sacrifice. The person can die to themselves only in union with the humanity of Jesus on the cross.

Paschal mystery and 'wisdom of the cross'

The paschal mystery is a term we use to refer to Jesus' own passover: his cross and resurrection. Jesus achieved the fullness of life by embracing the cross, offering himself in loving obedience to the Father, even in death. The cross stands for a loving trust placed in the Father. It states that we will allow God freedom in our lives. The cross is the instrument of detachment and the symbol of an unquestioning generosity in allowing God the freedom to decide according to his will. The one who embraces it, not out of despair or lack of choice but willingly, has gone beyond all the attachment and resistance offered by the internal and external forces that dominate a person.[61]

John was very much at home with the dialectic patterns found in the writings of Paul. We often come across opposing terms which seem to negate each other, like life-death, light-darkness, presence-absence, low-high, joy-sorrow, spirit-flesh, old self-new self, and so on. Among these paradoxes, that of the cross is the supreme one. Its paradox is visually presented by its design itself, a horizontal line intersecting a vertical line. The cross is the victory over self. It is the victory of humanity as well as the victory of God. On the cross, the self-protecting force of human consciousness was transcended. Chapter seven of the second book of *Ascent* contains John's major exposition of the cross of Christ in its relationship to the experience of *nada*. He begins his treatment of this theme by quoting the passage from Mark's Gospel, where Jesus says that if anyone wishes to be his disciple, he must renounce himself, take up his cross, and follow him, for whoever wants to save their life must loose it.[62] John interprets this text spiritually, as referring to a dispossession and annihilation of the spirit, in the following words:

> They think denial of self in worldly matters is sufficient without annihilation and purification in the spiritual domain. It happens that, when some of this solid, perfect food (the annihilation of all sweetness in God – the pure spiritual cross and nakedness of Christ's poverty of spirit) is offered them in dryness, distaste and trial, they run from it as from death and wander about in search only of sweetness and delightful communications from God. Such an attitude is not the hallmark of self-denial and nakedness of spirit but the indication of spiritual sweet tooth. Through this kind of conduct they become, spiritually speaking, enemies of the cross of Christ (Phil 3:18).[63]

In this text, John equates annihilation, purification, nakedness, and self-denial with the cross of Christ. The poverty of spirit achieved through the embrace of the cross is for him the experience of *nada*. The cross of Christ is, for John, the symbol of the complete spiritual death of the senses and the spirit, which he considers essential for the union with God and as constituting the experience of nothingness. He explains:

> at the moment of his death he was certainly annihilated in his soul, without any consolation or relief, since the Father had left him that way in innermost aridity in the lower part. He was thereby compelled to cry out: *My God, my God, why have you forsaken me?* (Mt 27:46). This was the most extreme abandonment, sensitively, that he had suffered in his life. And by it he accomplished the most marvellous work of his whole life... The Lord achieved this, as I say, at the moment in which he was most annihilated in all things: in his human nature, by dying; and in spiritual help and consolation from his Father, for he was forsaken by his Father at that time, so as to pay the debt fully and bring man to union with God.[64]

John builds his theory of salvation through the cross upon the text from Matthew's Gospel that we have just seen. On the cross, through the extreme self-abandonment, Jesus demonstrated oneness with his Father. He had no will of his own other than that of his Father. When Jesus abandoned himself totally, what remained was his Father's will. Union with God is to be achieved according to the same pattern. The spiritual death of the person, that is, the ultimate experience of *nada*, is the moment of union or salvation. John describes the deep impact of the horrific spiritual abandonment on an individual as follows:

> because of the solitude and desolation this night causes, the individuals in this state find neither consolation nor support in any doctrine or spiritual master... Their helplessness is even greater because of the little they can do in this situation. They resemble one who is imprisoned in a dark dungeon, bound hands and feet, and able neither to move nor see nor feel any favour from heaven or earth. They remain in this condition until their spirit is humbled, softened, and purified, until it becomes so delicate, simple and refined that it can be one with the Spirit of God, according to the degree of union of love that God, in his mercy desires to grant.[65]

Kenosis tells us something about 'God the Father', too. If Jesus, the true image of God, displayed *kenosis* as his fundamental characteristic, his 'self-emptying nature' must therefore be a characteristic feature of the divinity he inherited from his Father. God communicates himself in the *kenosis* of Christ. The essence of this communication is love: "For God so loved the world that he gave his only Son" (Jn 3:16). This love of God for the world, which is revealed in the *kenosis* of the cross, is also found in the *kenosis* of love at the core of creation that is in turn an expression of the eternal love that is God. Jesus' *kenosis* is a manifestation, a revelation of the *kenosis* of God. The essential quality of the *kenosis* of both the Father and the Son is love. The creative *kenosis* of the Father revealed itself in the redemptive *kenosis* of the Son.

Personal union

We come across the expression 'to unite' and its derivatives more than 500 times in John's works. If we add the words with a similar meaning, and parallel expressions like 'transformation', 'to make equal', 'to join' and so on, the number exceeds a thousand. According to John, everything in spiritual life can be expressed by one idea – the union of love. In the state of union, where nothing belonging to the ego exists except a loving awareness of God, "the soul receives God's self-communication passively, just as people receive light passively without doing anything else but keeping their eyes open."[66] In *Ascent*, John clarifies this concept: "Here we have the reason for stating that two wills become one. And this one will is God's will, which also becomes the soul's... in order for a soul to reach union with God through its will and love, it must first be freed from every appetite, however slight."[67] In order to make his point clear, John uses the example of sexual union:

> Just as in the consummation of carnal marriage there are two in one flesh, as Sacred Scripture points out (Gn. 2:24), so also when spiritual marriage between God and the soul is consummated, there are two natures in one spirit and love, as St Paul says in making this same comparison: *Whoever is joined to the Lord becomes one spirit with him* (1 Cor 6:17).[68]

John identifies the 'children of God' with those who are transformed in God and united to him.[69] Previously the person's experiences had a natural origin. The intellect, which understood everything by means of the natural senses, begins to be moved by the supernatural light, bypassing the senses as a result of the new life. Accordingly, the human intellect becomes one with God's intellect. The will, which previously loved with a natural affection, is now changed, moved by the Holy Spirit; the person's will is one with God's. The memory that was filled with images and fantasies created from the raw materials collected by the senses from the creatures, is changed through a divine forgetfulness, so as to be filled with thoughts of eternity:

> For the soul, like a true daughter of God, is moved in all by the Spirit of God, as St Paul teaches in saying that those who are moved by the Spirit of God are children of God himself (Rom 8:14). Accordingly, the intellect of this soul is God's intellect; its will is God's will; its memory is the memory of God; and its delight is God's delight; and although the substance of this soul is not the substance of God, since it cannot undergo a substantial conversion into him, it has become God through participation, being united to and absorbed in him, as it is in this state.[70]

Having 'the mind of Christ' is the most reliable sign of union with him. Freedom and spontaneity are the characteristic marks of those who have the "mind of Christ" (1 Cor 2:16). A slavish fear of the Creator or a slavish attachment to creation holds us back from learning to see ourselves as children of God. To be moved by the Spirit is a precondition for being a child of God, since it is the Spirit that enables us to call God "Abba! Father!"(Rom 8:15; Gal 4:4-7). To possess the Spirit of Christ means we are bold enough to say 'yes' to God even at the risk of losing our own life. To have the mind of Christ means to be confident and humble enough to give up our own will and be generous and obedient enough to give up our own life (Phil 2:5-11; Rom 8:17-18). The readiness of Paul to be cut off from Christ for the salvation of his fellow Jews (Rom 9:3) is a clear expression of this. It also implies a state of peace with God. John points out that real love consists not in great "feelings" but in great "sacrifice".[71] When we possess the mind of Christ we no longer rebel or feel at odds with God. We pass from the state of disobedience to the state of collaboration with God, living in reconciliation, peace and gratitude towards him.

God is love and love is essentially self-giving. Christ emptied himself because, as we have already noted, self-giving is in the nature of God. The Father gave his only

Son to the world because it was natural for him to do that. Self-giving is the essence of God. Jesus proved his divinity through his self-gift at Bethlehem and on Calvary. As the person starts the process of self-giving, the process of *kenosis* begins. Total *kenosis*, that is, entry into *nada*, is an entry into God's nature which is self-giving. Total *kenosis* reveals pure divinity; God is *nada* and *nada* is God, because *nada* is the unconditional, self-negating love. In John's view, both the human aspiration for God and the readiness of God to take humanity upon himself come together and are thoroughly fulfilled. This also makes clear the nature of the self-emptying of Jesus as both a divine act and a human act that raises him to the realm of the divine. Just as the self-emptying of Jesus was total, the person who desires to be like Jesus has to empty the ego-self completely. A complete submission to God results in two natures becoming united in one spirit, to the extent that such a person can now claim like Paul, "it is no longer I who live, but it is Christ lives in me" (Gal 2:20). In such a state it is the Spirit of Christ that dominates, leads and guides:

> This is the meaning of St Paul's affirmation: *Vivo autem, iam non ego; vivit vero in me Christus* (I live, now not I, but Christ lives in me) (Gal 2:20). In saying, "I live, now not I," he meant that even though he had life it was not his because he was transformed in Christ, and it was divine more than human. He consequently asserts that he does not live but Christ lives in him. In accord with this likeness and transformation, we can say that his life and Christ's were one life through union of love. This transformation into divine life will be effected perfectly in heaven in all those who merit the vision of God. Transformed in God, these blessed souls will live the life of God and not their own life – although, indeed, it will be their own because God's life will be theirs. Then they will truly proclaim: We live now not we, but God lives in us. Although transformation in this life can be what it was in St Paul, it still cannot be perfect and complete even though the soul reaches such transformation of love as is found in the spiritual marriage, the highest state attainable in this life.[72]

Communal deification

John traces the origin of humanity to the Trinity.[73] Creation was made in the image and likeness of the eternal Word, so that it might resemble its future bridegroom.[74] In John's understanding, creation implicitly and explicitly is linked to Christ since it is totally dependent on him (1 Cor 8:6). Creation was planned with a view to the future incarnation of the Word; the Father intends to 'propose' to creation, when she is grown-up and ready for him. It was the love for the bride that motivated the Word to undertake *kenosis*. The bride through the same path of *kenosis* has to prove her love and likeness to her beloved. Only through transformation into Christ does creation achieve its meaning and purpose: "he chose us in Christ, before the foundation of the world to be holy and blameless before him in love" (Eph 1:4). John further clarifies the ultimate destiny of humanity in his commentary on *Canticle*:

> This is the adoption of the children of God, who will indeed declare to God what the very Son said to the Eternal Father through St John: *All my things are yours, and yours are mine* (Jn 17:10). He says this by essence, since he is the natural Son of God, and we say it by participation, since we are adopted children. He declared this not only for himself, the Head, but for his whole mystical body, the Church.[75]

Canticle speaks of the union of human nature with God's Word that took place in Jesus and made possible the corresponding union of all human beings with God.[76] This destiny of humanity is a common, or better, communal, one – "all the members of the body, though many, are one body" (1 Cor 12:12; cf. Rom 12:5). The deification we saw before, is a communal event. Each person becomes part of the mystical body and, humbly taking their place in the communal life of ultimate Reality, enjoys the experience of union.[77] Paul observes that this unity of the mystical body depends on the mutual *kenosis* of the members of the community as they participate in the death and resurrection of Christ (2 Cor 4:10-11).

Thomas Aquinas and the theological foundations of John's writings

John attended the University of Salamanca, whose theological syllabus, like that of any Catholic university in the sixteenth century, was grounded in Scholastic theology. The best of the Scholastic tradition was represented by the works of Thomas Aquinas, and John expressed his own doctrine in terms of Thomas' well-established, mature and refined thought.[78] The Scholastic tradition as a whole fundamentally followed the Greek philosopher Aristotle, who was not inclined to ignore the visible world and things that could be seen and touched. To complement this approach John turned, as in fact Thomas himself had, to the Augustinian tradition and the ideas of Pseudo-Dionysius, which had more in common with the ideas of Plato and his later elaborators (especially the Neoplatonists) who tended to forget about the world around us that our senses perceive, and to value the more mystical and invisible aspect of our lives. Indeed, John may well have had first-hand knowledge of the works of Augustine, Pseudo-Dionysius and Thomas Aquinas, which enabled him to lay a secure philosophical and theological foundation for the path to union with God he was to mark out.

To grasp the importance of the ideas of Thomas Aquinas in the mystical writings of John we need to consider three principles established by the dominican as the basis for any understanding of the relationship between God and man.[79] The first principle is that God alone depends on no other being for his existence, whereas all other beings do. The difference between God and everything else is that God alone exists independently, while all these other things are dependent upon him. This is not to say that we humans and the world around us are mere products of our minds or of our feelings; both have actual existence, called to relate to the 'being' of God.

Secondly, Thomas teaches that faith is distinct from

reason. To believe and trust in God is not the same as being able to prove the existence of the God of the Bible through one's own reason. Reason, thought Thomas, can lead us to prove the existence of a God, as will be seen very shortly, but is unable to plumb the depths of the incomprehensible mystery of his 'being'. God has given human beings intellectual ability precisely to help them to 'feel after him and find him,' so that any search for truth is in essence a search after God, who builds upon our natural powers of discernment by revealing himself as consistent with them. Thomas argues that reason (and hence philosophy, which is a disciplined use of reason), unaided by revelation, *does* lead us to an understanding of God as one, simple, eternal, good, who exists without depending on any other being – but draws a clear limit to the claims of reason to be able to lead us directly to God. Reason is able to reach certain conclusions, but they do not describe the God in whom Christians believe. There has to be an initiative from God himself – which we call revelation – to tell us more, and to this revelation we respond with faith. Reason, therefore, cannot bring the seeker to the fundamental Christian truths about God which lie beyond reason in the realm of revelation, such as the Trinity, the incarnation, the resurrection and so on. Such teachings, though not contrary to reason, cannot be established by it. They reach us through revelation, embodied in the Scriptures and in the consistent tradition and teaching of the Church. In order to come to a fuller knowledge of God, the person who seeks God, has to believe that what is presented to them through the history of God's self-disclosure – in the Old Testament and supremely in Jesus of Nazareth – is true.

Thirdly, Thomas maintains that any knowledge we possess has something to do with the world outside our own minds. There is an objective world outside us and beyond us, which can be explored by means of the senses. Similarly, God is also an (infinite) 'being', but, since he is beyond the reach of sense-perception, by which the intellect gathers information, we have to depend upon his self-revelation for obtaining knowledge regarding him (or better, how he acts) and accept it in faith. The acquisition of knowledge concerning creation depends on how deeply we involve our senses in the matters about which we want to acquire knowledge. The acquisition of knowledge regarding God depends on how deeply the person dissociates themselves from the creation and turns to God who reveals his truths. Different people are at different stages in their pilgrimage of faith.[80]

These fundamental ideas of Thomas Aquinas lay the theological foundation of John's mystical teachings. This following of Thomas has two important consequences for John's analysis of the path to union with God. Firstly, John assumes a radical break between the uncreated, infinite, independent being of God and the created, finite, dependent being of everything else that exists. This means that anyone who aspires to attain union with God, must set their heart on the being of God and not be distracted by the love of created things. The choice lies between a union of love with creation and a union of love with God. This being the case, it follows that all human knowledge and abilities are really just ignorance compared with the infinite wisdom of God and are, therefore, not appropriate means of seeking union with God. Furthermore, John rejects the pursuit of worldly desires and the attachment to the natural and the supernatural goods on the path of union with God. If we become attached to goods we shall be enslaved by them. However, detachment from goods alone will not lead anyone to union with God. We have to enter *nada* and remain in it as if in a 'dark night'. This 'dark night experience' is in reality, the absence of rational under-standing, a life in faith.[81]

Secondly, John assumes that God's grace operates in created things in accordance with their nature. Such treatment of his creatures reveals God's graciousness and respect: he leads us forward, step by step, to union with him, loving us even more than we love him, and brings us to perfection in a way appropriate to our human nature. Our human nature is not put aside, but transformed. We are not called to reject our nature, which is God-given, but to free it from the bondage that prevents us from uniting with God.

Spiritual foundations of John's life and vision

John was familiar with the spiritual writings of his contemporaries from France, the Netherlands, Flanders, Germany and Italy, as well as with the writings of the Fathers of the Church – both eastern and western; but his deepest familiarity was with Scripture.[82] His knowledge of Scripture was such that his fellow religious believed it was infused.[83] Unlike his contemporaries, John was not in the habit of quoting profusely from sources other than the Bible. The few quotations from the Fathers that appear in his works are taken from the Breviary, the prayer book of the Church. With the exception of Augustine, Pseudo-Dionysius, Bernard, Gregory, and Thomas Aquinas, we do not come across the names of many authors in his writings. His method of quoting was to integrate the ideas of others into his stream of thought without giving any reference to their source. The probable reason is that he was not working in a methodical way. He wrote at the request of some of his associates to explain the nuances of his poetry and to assist them in their struggle to attain 'spiritual poverty'. Being well initiated into the philosophy, theology, and spirituality of his period, which he absorbed, assimilated and systematised on the basis of his personal experiences, John was not a 'solitary bird' singing his 'mystical songs' from the 'roof' of his mystical experience. He was a part of the long mystical tradition of humanity. A Benedictine of Stanbrook Abbey points out:

What he did do was to clear away the long, often contradictory
digressions and repetitions of the medievalists, separate the
essential from non essential, and in short do for mystical theology
much of what St Thomas Aquinas did for the subject [theology]
in general.[84]

Influence of the writings of the Fathers of the Church on John

The first difficulty we encounter when assessing the
influence of the Church Fathers on John is the absence of
references and footnotes in his writings. Nevertheless,
influences there are, and we will try to discern the presence
of three of them. Inadequate though this treatment is, it
should serve to introduce us to some of his more important
sources.

Augustine's writings such as *Confessions, Homilies on
Psalms, Homilies on the First Epistle of John,* tell of his
mystical experiences and his ideas concerning mysticism. It
was to his writings that almost all the western mystics of
the later centuries appealed for the confirmation of their
disputed ideas.[85] John depended heavily on Augustine for
the development of his ideas concerning the person's
contemplative and ecstatic experiences in their ascent to
God. Furthermore, John saw that Augustine's understanding of the nature of the human person as the image of
the triune God made such experiences possible.[86]

Gregory of Nyssa followed Origen in his allegorical
method of interpreting the Scriptures. His *Life of Moses,*
his homilies on the *Song of Songs,* and so on, laid the
foundations for John's own writings. Gregory's mystical
concepts like 'the night', 'the dark vision', 'the ascent to
God through successive stages of purification', and the
like, reappear in the writings of John with a new splendour
and majesty. In Gregory's writings John found a model to
describe the journey of the believer to God. Gregory,
following the example of Origen, and taking inspiration

from similar biblical texts and Greek philosophical speculations, sketched out in his *Life of Moses,* a model describing progress along the mystical path. Through numerous homilies, dedicated to the mystical interpretation of the *Song of Songs,* he showed how the book speaks both of Christ's love for the Church and the love between the human person and the divine bridegroom.

The writings of the pseudonymous author we generally refer to as **Pseudo-Dionysius,** probably a Syrian monk of the late fifth or early sixth centuries, have been enormously influential in the history of mysticism. His influence on western Christian thought was great, especially from the ninth century onwards, and his writings were subject to numerous translations and commentaries. He is one of the few authors John mentions by name.

Down through the centuries, the ambiguous passages found in the works of Pseudo-Dionysius were diligently interpreted in orthodox terms and were successfully proposed as an authoritative programme of the ascent to God.[87] His treatise, *Mystical Theology,* presents his views on spiritual progress. Here he develops an *apophatic* or 'negative' spirituality based on Moses' experience of God on the Mount Sinai. Moses, in his ascent to the vision of God, had to pass through different stages. As the ideal mystic, Moses had to undergo, first, purification (*katharsis*). As a result he gained contemplation (*theoria*) of the place (not the essence) of God and finally attained union (*henosis*).[88] The book begins with the narration of Moses ascending into the 'cloud of unknowing' on the Mount Sinai and concludes with the principle of negating all presumed attributes of God.

The interpretation of Scriptural symbolism found in Pseudo-Dionysius marries positive and negative approaches. He insists on the need for transcending both superficial and 'lofty' ideas concerning God through a continuous negation until the person is able to silently approach the ineffable and transcendent God, who is beyond all speech and thought. According to Pseudo-Dionysius, the primary purpose of symbols is to uplift the faithful from the realm of sense-perception to that of the intellect. This ascent involves two steps. The first is the right interpretation of the symbols so that one may move from the symbols to the concepts symbolised through them. The second step is the negation and abandonment of all such concepts due to their inadequacy. As the supreme cause of all, God is to an extent revealed in all of the created order and in human knowledge. But transcending all and dwelling in the 'Divine Darkness', God is not fully revealed in creation or in any human concept. God, therefore, is known through both 'knowing' and 'unknowing'. Even the most sublime concepts of God, for example, God as the 'eternal light', or 'Goodness', or God's unity and Trinity, and so on, stand merely at the limited pinnacle of human language and thought. Ultimately, they too must be recognised as deficient and negated.

The final goal of the Pseudo-Dionysian negative way is 'deification' or *theosis*, which could be translated as the maximum possible union with God. In the fifth chapter of *Mystical Theology*, the negative way reaches the point at which all intelligible and conceptual truths are negated. At this decisive point, even the denial is to be left behind as incapable of expressing the divine goal of this ascent. Negation of the conceptual realm means negating and transcending even the concept of negation.[89] Negations are themselves negated. Thus, the final step culminates in complete silence. The progressive steps of affirmation and negation cease to be efficacious in the ultimate arena of the divine encounter where silence is the right attitude:

> Here, renouncing all that the mind may conceive, wrapped entirely in the intangible and invisible, he belongs completely to him who is beyond everything. Here, being neither oneself nor someone else, one is supremely united by a completely unknowing inactivity of all knowledge, and knows beyond the mind by knowing nothing.[90]

Influence of medieval authors on John

There is a long list of known and important medieval authors who contributed towards the formation of John's perspective. A thorough consideration of the extent to which they might have influenced John is beyond the scope of this present book. Of all the many figures we could have chosen, including Bernard of Clairvaux, Hugh and Richard of St Victor, John Ruysbroeck and John Tauler, we will look briefly at Meister Eckhart, a surprising influence, perhaps.

Although the full orthodoxy of the teachings of the great German speculative mystic **Meister Eckhart** is still debated, some of his concepts may well have influenced John. Eckhart held the view that God is 'all' and creatures are 'pure nothingness'. Whereas God inherently possesses being, creatures do not possess it, but receive it derivatively. Outside God, there is pure nothingness, that is, beings receive their existence from God. Eckhart specifies four stages in the progress of the soul towards God: dissimilarity, similarity, identity, and breakthrough. Eckhart calls 'Godhead' the origin of all things including 'God-the Creator', and asserts that, God and the Godhead are as distinct as heaven and earth. In the last of the four stages the soul has moved beyond God-the Creator. God-the Creator exists only in relation with the creation. Once there is no more creation, God-the Creator too will cease to exist. There will remain only Godhead who contains God as well as creation as it was in the beginning. For Meister Eckhart, God exists as God only when creatures invoke him. Therefore, identity with God is not enough. Humans must live 'without why'. They must seek nothing, not even God. Abandoning all things without abandoning God is not abandoning anything. By means of a continuous and increasing detachment one should break through into the desert of the Godhead. This idea can be read as genuinely Christian: certainly on a spiritual level it retraces, for the believer, the *kenotic* way of the cross of Christ. Though not acknowledged, the passionate spirit of detachment seen in John's writings is very much in tune with Eckhart's spirituality.

Sufi mysticism and Spain

It is possible to argue that Spanish Christian mysticism owes a great deal to Sufism. One author, after comparing John's work with those of the Persian and Spanish Sufis asserts: "St John of the Cross is a synthesis of Spanish mysticism, both Christian and Muslim."[91] By the middle of the sixteenth century, Medina del Campo, where from 1551 John spent his childhood, was populated with a considerable number of *Moriscos*. John certainly had plenty of opportunities to encounter Muslims and Sufism. These *Moriscos* conserved a good deal of their cultural heritage. In Granada, where John lived for six years and wrote almost all his great works, *Moriscos* constituted the major part of the population. The monastery in which John lived was situated near Alhambra, the greatest of Hispano-Muslim monuments. The other monastery where he used to stay whenever he was in Calle Elvira was also adjacent to another *Morisco* quarter – Albaicin. Thus, while in Granada, John was literally surrounded by *Moriscos* and by monuments of the Hispano-Muslim past. There are historical documents pointing towards the existence of clandestine as well as professed Muslims in Granada even after John's time. Among these Muslims, the 'Mooress of Ubeda', regarded as the follower of the doctrine of al-Ghazali, was specially known for her saintliness. It was at Ubeda that John lived for the first time after arriving in Andalusia, and it was there that he died.

An examination of the beliefs of the Illuminists (*alumbrados*) reveals the influence of Sufism on Christian believers. Originating in western Andalusia, the heartland of Hispano-Muslim Sufism, Illuminism appears to be a degenerate form of Sufi mysticism, and it plagued Christian Spain in the sixteenth century. Even John was accused of Illuminism by his opponents. In his own writings John often speaks of God as the 'Beloved', almost in the same way and often using the same words as did the Sufis. The great Spanish Sufi, Muhyi al-Din Ibn al-Arabi (1165-1240) insisted on the oneness of being (*wahdat at-wujud*). Ibn Abbad of Ronda (fourteenth century), named one of his principal works *Dark Night of the Soul* and preached renunciation in forceful terms similar to those we find later in the works of John of the Cross.

John's poetic style is without parallel among Christian mystics, but reveals a great similarity with that of the Sufi mystics of Persia. The similarity of the titles of John's works with that of al-Ghazali (e.g., *Ascent to the Court of Sanctity, Ascent of the Pilgrims, Niche for Lights*) is remarkable. The devastation of Persia by Mongolian invaders in the thirteenth and fourteenth centuries caused a migration of Sufis and Dervishes to the kingdom of Granada. Ibn Batuta (fourteenth century), the great Persian traveller, tells us that he personally met in Granada Dervishes from Tabriz, Samarcand, Konia, and India.

Conclusion

Our examination of John's *nada* spirituality thus far has revealed the complexity of its foundations, and their firmness. It is also clear that this *nada* spirituality is tightly anchored to his own real spiritual and life experiences; and, as we would expect, the political situation of sixteenth-century Spain, and the religious and spiritual trends of that period contributed substantially towards its development. In John's writings we see three things fused harmoniously together: all that happened in his life, all that is perennial in human nature, all that is basic to Christianity.

John found in the Old and New Testaments the

authority for his *nada* spirituality. He found the fullest
expression of the mystical aspect of Christianity in John's
Gospel and in the letters of Paul. In the former, particularly
in the farewell discourse (chapters 14-16), Jesus speaks of
his impending death and of his return in the Spirit to unite
himself with his followers. In the prayer of Jesus in chapter
17 there is a vision of a union in which all who are one
with Christ partake in his perfect union with the Father.
This union has its highest realisation in the *kenosis* of Jesus.
Paul envisages this *kenosis* as the supreme example left by
Jesus and furthermore the future.

When John turned to the mystical writings of Gregory
of Nyssa, he found a model to describe the believer's
journey to God. But great as Gregory's effect was on John,
it is perhaps the teachings of Pseudo-Dionysius that had
the profoundest influence on the shaping of John's spiritual
thinking. In the *Mystical Theology* and other works,
Dionysius emphasised the ineffability of God (the Divine
Darkness) and proposed the *apophatic* or negative approach
to God. Through a gradual process of ascension from
material things to spiritual realities and an eventual stripping
away of all created beings in unknowing, the person arrives
at union with God who transcends all beings and all
knowledge and dwells in darkness.

Taking a lead from his predecessors, John proposed a
detailed study of the stages of the ascent of the person to
God. John was profoundly convinced of the nothingness
of creation in comparison with God, and the loss through
sin of the pristine likeness that the human person once had
to God and of its creation in his image (Gen 1:26). He
insisted on the role of love as the power that unites us to
God (1 Cor 6:17). He combined these primitive Jewish-
Christian themes with the Greek speculative emphasis on
the incomprehensibility of God. He knew that this concept
of the unintelligibility of God finds a strong resonance in
many texts of the Old and New Testaments, which affirm
that the God of Abraham and the Father of Jesus can never

be fully known. He found Scriptural authorisation for the Greek emphasis on the vision or contemplation (*theoria*) of God as the goal of human blessedness in the sixth Beatitude, "Blessed are the pure in heart, for they will see God" (Mt 5:8). In the New Testament's emphasis on becoming the sons of God (Gal 4:5ff), in those passages which talk about the call to share in the divine nature (2 Pet 1:4), and in the concept of deification he found a way of understanding the transformation worked on human nature by God's action.

In this chapter we have examined the numerous currents of religious experience and thought circulating in John's world and seen how well noted he was in the philosophical, theological and scriptural disciplines of his day. This formation equipped him superbly to describe his journey along the *nada* path as he encountered the deepest realities of human existence and the Christian faith.

NOTES

1 F. Ruiz (ed.). *God Speaks in the Night: The Life, Times, and Teachings of St John of the Cross* (tr., K. Kavanaugh), (Washington: ICS Publications, 1991), v-vi.

2 A. E. Peers, *Spirit of Flame: A Study of St John of the Cross* (London: SCM Press, 1979), 104.

3 *2A* 4,4; 8,4; *3A* 12,1; *2N* 9,4; *C* 38,6.

4 *2A* 28,1.

5 For a full account of the trials undergone by John, cf. "John of the Cross and God's Absence", A. Cugno, *St John of the Cross: The Life and Thought of a Christian Mystic* (tr., B. Wall), (London: Burns & Oates, 1982), 42-50.

6 *The Collected Works of St John of the Cross* (tr., K. Kavanaugh and O. Rodriguez), 23.

7 R.P. Hardy, *Search for nothing: The life of St John of the Cross* (New York: Cross Roads, 1982), 7, 9, 13; G.M. Bruno, *St John of the Cross* (New York: Sheed & Ward, 1932), 3; J. de Crisógono, *The life St John of the Cross* (tr., K. Pond), (London: Longmans, 1958), 9.

8 F. Ruiz, *God Speaks in the Night*, 17-18, 93-117; O. Rodriguez, *Saint John of the Cross – The Nightingale of God* (Rome: Teresianum, 1990), 12-13; Chrysogonus, *Saint John of the Cross: His Life* (tr., Stanislaus),

(Vemsur: Tersian Press, 1985), 10-36; S. Payne (ed.), *John of the Cross*, Carmelite Studies II (Trivandrum: Carmel Publishing Centre, 1995), 21.

9 Corominas, *Diccionario Critico etimologico de la lengua Castellana* (Madrid: Editorial de Gregos, 1954), 489-491.

10 *1A* 4,3.

11 'Dark Night', stanza 4.

12 *A* Prologue, 8.

13 *LF* 1,27-28.

14 *C* 35,6.

15 *1N* 11,3.

16 *1A* 14,2.

17 J. de Crisógono, *The Life of St John of the Cross*, p. 281.

18 E.E. Larkin, "The Dark Night of John of the Cross", *The Way* 14 (1974), 15.

19 *2A* 26,4.

20 *2N* 16,7.

21 *2N* 16,13.

22 *2N* 19,4.

23 *2N* 6,1.

24 *2N* 6,1.

25 *2N* 6,5.

26 *LF* 1,9-10.

27 *2N* 4,1.

28 'Dark Night,' Stanza 4.

29 *2N* 17,6.

30 *C* 26,4.

31 F. Ruiz, *San Giovanni della Croce: Mistico e Maestro* (Bologna: EBD, 1991), 47.

32 F. Ruiz, *San Giovanni della Croce*, 48.

33 *1A* 5,6.

34 *1A* 5.

35 *1A* 5,5-8.

36 *3A* 16,1.

37 *1A* 5,2; *2A* 6,4; *3A* 7,2; *LF* 3,46.

38 *1A* 5,2.

39 *LF* 3,46.

40 *3A* 17-45.

41 *2A* 6,4.

42 *3A* 35,4; 36,1.

43 *C* 20-21,15.

44 D. Centner, "Christian Freedom and the Nights of St John of the Cross", in J. Sullivan (ed.), *Contemporary Psychology and Carmel*, Carmelite Studies (Washington DC: ICS Publications, 1982), 51-52.

45 S.L. Lund, "Desire in St John of the Cross", *Spiritual Life* 31/2

(1985), 93.

46 *2A* 7,11.

47 *1N* 10,1.

48 H.U. von Balthasar, *Prayer* (tr., G. Harrison), (San Francisco: Ignatius Press, 1986), 55.

49 *2A* 7,11.

50 *C* 29,3.

51 N. Cummins, *Freedom to Rejoice* (London: Harper Collins Religious, 1991), 18.

52 *1N* 1,1.

53 *2A* 7,11.

54 N. Cummins, *Freedom to Rejoice*, 25.

55 P. John Paul II, *Fides et Ratio*, n.11.

56 *C* 39,5.

57 H.U. von Balthasar, *Christian Meditation* (tr., M.T. Skerry), (San Francisco: Ignatius Press, 1989), 57.

58 *C* 36,5.

59 Cf. E. Stein, *The Science of the Cross: A Study of St John of the Cross* (Chicago: Henry Regnery Company, 1960), 9.

60 W. McGreal, *John of the Cross*, Fount Christian Thinkers Series (London: Fount, 1996), 62.

61 W. McGreal, *John of the Cross*, 58.

62 *2A* 7,4.

63 *2A* 7,5.

64 *2A* 7,11.

65 *2N* 7,3.

66 *2A* 15,2.

67 *1A* 11,3.

68 *C* 22,3.

69 *3A* 2,7-16.

70 *LF* 2,34.

71 cf. *Sayings* 16.

72 *C* 12,8.

73 'Romance 3', verse 1.

74 *C* 39,4; 23,3-6.

75 *C* 36,5.

76 *C* 37,3.

77 E. Underhill, *Mysticism* (New York: Image Books, 1990), 425.

78 T. Merton, *The Ascent to Truth* (Ken: Burns & Oates, 1994), 89.

79 J.P. Torrell, *Saint Thomas Aquinas: The Person and his Work*, Vol. 1 (tr., R. Royal), (Washington, D.C.: The Catholic University of America Press, 1996), 148-159.

80 D.B. Tillyer, *Union with God: the teaching of St John of the Cross* (London & Oxford: Mowbray, 1984), 26-30.

81 *1A* 2,1.

82 A Benedictine of Stanbrook Abbey, *Medieval Mystical Tradition and Saint John of the Cross* (London: Burns & Oates, 1954), 23.
83 *Ibid.* 19.
84 *Ibid.* 24.
85 B. McGinn, *The Growth of Mysticism*, 231.
86 B. McGinn, *The Foundations*, 228-262.
87 B. McGinn, *The Foundations*, 158; J. Meyendorff, *A Study of Gregory Palamas* (London: Faith Press, 1964), 133, 185-192, 202-210.
88 B. McGinn, *The Foundations*, 172.
89 Cf. B. McGinn, *The Foundations*, 176.
90 Cf. C. Luibheid et al. (tr.), *Pseudo-Dionysius: The Complete Works,* The Classics of Western Spirituality (New York: Paulist Press, 1987), 137.
91 M. McClain, "Synthesis of Christian and Muslim Mysticism in Spain", *Nigerian Dialogue* 4/4 (1982), 21. See also 24-29.

TWO

NADA: THE PATH OF THE PERFECT SPIRIT

Introduction

Having looked at the way in which John used the term *nada*, it is now time to examine the path which John envisaged as leading to the state of *nada*: the 'Ascent of Mount Carmel'. This chapter, therefore, will describe this ascent, and the three paths we are offered, as understood by John and illustrated in his famous 'Sketch of Mount Carmel'. We will look first at the original sketch and then turn to the 'Redesigned Sketch of Mount Carmel'. The original sketch has been redesigned in order to clarify the arguments contained in this book, but this is not to imply that something is lacking in the original drawing or that it is in need of correction: the new design is essentially the same as John's sketch, though it does incorporate certain additional details which are fundamental to the discussion. The chapter continues with a short description of the four identifiable stages on the path of spiritual growth, namely birth, infancy, adulthood, and maturity. The remainder of the chapter will explore the three paths illustrated in the sketch, their motivating factors, pitfalls and consequences.

'Sketch of Mount Carmel' and its place in John's writings

John was not a professional writer.[1] His written works are not extensive: in all, about a thousand pages of prose and some thousand verses. The three poems that brought him fame ('Dark Night', 'Spiritual Canticle', and 'Living Flame of Love') total only 264 stanzas. The poems arose spontaneously: only gradually and with reluctance did John turn to writing prose. John lacked an inner urge to write prose, producing his commentaries on the poems at the request of his friends, the Carmelite friars and nuns and all those he was assisting spiritually. Although these writings were occasioned by particular circumstances, they possess a remarkable maturity and universality. His main prose compositions are *Ascent of Mount Carmel, Dark Night, Spiritual Canticle,* and *Living Flame of Love.* Also accredited to him are three short collections, namely: *Sayings of Light and Love, Precautions* and various letters. It is worth noting that in all these writings John shows that he was not a slavish follower of the traditional spiritual itineraries: at the heart of his system is the experience of 'night'. Basing himself on that experience, John demonstrates the right and perfect path that leads one to the 'nakedness of spirit'.

The 'Sketch of Mount Carmel' or 'Mount of Perfection' occupies a unique position in John's works.[2] This sketch gives us a concise summary of John's philosophical, theological and spiritual teachings. John himself considered that the 'Sketch of Mount Carmel' contained the essence of his teachings,[3] and so he placed it at the beginning of *Ascent* to serve as a summary of the doctrine contained in that treatise. We are told that he made copies of this visual synthesis of his instructions and distributed them among the Carmelite nuns of Beas and, later, among his own friars in Beaza and Granada. It is unfortunate that nobody seems to have requested him to write a commentary on his unique creation, as they did for his poetry. The commentaries he wrote on his poems brought to light the riches that lay hidden under the depths of his poetic skill; the simplicity and straightforward nature of his drawing might have deceived his contemporaries into thinking that no further explanation was required. The lack of a commentary on the sketch means that we do not possess a fully authoritative interpretation of it. Such an interpretation could only have deepened our understanding of the true path of *kenosis* that the sketch depicts. If we doubt this, then all we have to do is consider how much poorer Christian spirituality would be without the commentaries on John's poems!

John's 'Sketch of Mount Carmel' and its significance[4]

The 'Sketch of Mount Carmel' is a simple diagram representing the mount as a large oval with three paths at its base. The central path is identified as the path of 'nothing'. The word *nada* marks each of the stages along that path. The other two paths, designated as the paths of the imperfect spirits, indicate the paths of those who search for the goods of earth and goods of heaven. Both of these paths are dead ends and lead nowhere. John gives *nada* a central position in the sketch. The word *nada* is repeated nine times in the diagram. On the path of the perfect spirit that ascends towards the centre of the mount, the word *nada* is repeated six times in succession and at the summit he inscribed an emphatic "even on the mount nothing". Again at the left and right borders at the top of the drawing we read, "Glory matters nothing to me; Suffering matters nothing to me". The two series of six negations, the six material goods and the six spiritual goods, also provide ample proof of John's insistence on the centrality of *nada* on the path towards *el todo*. The paths of the imperfect spirits, taken by those who seek God through material or spiritual possessions, both lead to a dead end. The path of *nada* is the only path that leads in the right direction. John intentionally repeats the word *nada* seven times in the path of the perfect spirit, to show that it is the perfect path, since the number seven is the biblical number of perfection (Ps 12:6). Among the "instructions for climbing the summit, the high state of union", which occupy a fair amount of space at the bottom of the drawing, *nada* finds a prominent place. For John, the path to reach *el todo* is the negation of the desire for everything else, and the four concluding lines of those instructions express the freedom that the experience of *nada* can give.

'Redesigned Sketch of Mount Carmel' and its specific purpose[5]

The want of a commentary by John on the diagram can be in part rectified by gathering his ideas on *nada* from the commentaries he wrote on his poems: using these ideas we have redesigned the 'Sketch of Mount Carmel'. This redesigned sketch also depicts three paths: the path of the imperfect spirits who pursue the goods of earth; the path of the imperfect spirits who pursue the goods of heaven; and the path of the perfect spirit who walks on the path of *nada*. In the redesigned diagram, the paths of the imperfect spirits do not progress but remain on the horizontal plane, on the level of spiritual infancy with its possessiveness, attachments and insatiable desires. Those who decide to pursue these paths are not progressing any further towards God; instead, they become sidetracked and move further and further away from the perfect path. Their only means to advance towards God is to retrace their steps and enter the path of *nada*, the path that leads to spiritual adulthood and maturity.

As in the original diagram, the path on the right side represents the search for knowledge, possessions, joy, rest, and consolation; the path on the left the acquisition of knowledge, glory, joy, rest, and consolation; the middle path full immersion in *nada*. In the redesigned diagram all three paths have a common origin, but on the ascending middle path four stages are demarcated. They are (following the normal pattern of human growth), the stages of birth, infancy, adulthood and maturity. The 'path of the Spirit' opens up as the result of a conversion; a strong desire for God 'fires' the soul and makes it ready to 'die to the old self and its insipid paths' so as to go out in search of God, the divine Lover.[6] This is the point of entry into the supernatural realm, characterised by a strong desire for God and a deeply-felt turning from the 'profane'. This initial stage is called 'spiritual birth'. The person who is 'born' spiritually, through the continual exercise in the spiritual life, slowly begins to grow and in this process acquires various virtues, reaching the second stage, namely, spiritual infancy, which is a realm of desire, attachment, and possession.[7] There is a real danger that a spiritual person may remain in the stage of spiritual infancy until their death. Unfortunately, only very rarely do people outgrow the stage of infancy and reach maturity. Most spiritual persons prefer to remain as 'infants', collecting goods until the bell tolls for them, rather than attaining the adult state of nothingness! Spiritual infants have four choices at their disposal: the first is to turn back to the old ways of the world; the second, to turn right and pursue the path that offers the goods of earth; the third, to turn left and seek after the goods of heaven; the fourth and most difficult is to leave spiritual infancy by setting out along the path of *nada*. Moving along the *nada* path the spiritual infants begin to grow into adulthood through self-emptying, eventually attaining 'nakedness of spirit' in spiritual maturity.

Stages of spiritual growth

Because of his conviction that God is the 'primary mover',[8] John was always very reluctant to present a detailed programme of asceticism for attaining the freedom or "poverty of the spirit",[9] as he often calls it. In his view, God takes the lead in the process of radical purification, and the human role is to allow him to operate by willingly accepting his ongoing work of purification and all its consequences. Personal effort, however intense and essential, does not achieve the radical stripping demanded by God. God's intervention is experienced passively by the subject, and is beyond the realm of human effort.[10] Human endeavour and God's action are parallel and simultaneous; the experiences a person undergoes during this co-operative effort to break the chains of the three primordial enemies, namely, the world, the flesh, and the devil, John calls night. A journey through the dark night enables the person to bring these three great enemies under control.

Spiritual birth

A person is said to be born spiritually when they are disillusioned by the attractions of the world, developing a strong affinity for spiritual matters.[11] This does not mean that such a person is beyond the reach of the world, the flesh, and the devil. The individual, though in a different realm, is still under their domain, and is still vulnerable to their many traps as before. Both types of goods can attract a person who has been born spiritually, but the attraction such a person feels towards material or natural goods and spiritual or supernatural goods will always be driven by a spiritual motivation. John divides imperfect spiritual persons into two groups, based on the types of goods they are attracted to: they are, the imperfect spirits who seek to possess goods of earth and the imperfect spirits who seek to possess goods of heaven. John calls them imperfect spirits because, though they are spiritually born and have decided to follow the path of the spirit, they have failed to turn away from the goods they encounter along the path to perfection.

Spiritual infancy

The beginner or spiritual infant, who starts their journey on the path towards perfection is treated like a babe by God, the "heavenly mother".[12] God treats the beginner like a mother, who warms her child with her body, nurses it with milk and food, and carries and caresses it in her arms. But once the beginner has made a certain amount of progress on the path of perfection, God alters his mode of dealing with them. John likens the way God deals with this more seasoned traveller to a mother who withholds her caresses and hides her love from her growing infant. She rubs bitter aloes on her breast and sets the child down from her arms letting it walk on its own feet so that it may put aside the habits of childhood and grow accustomed to the ways of the adults. Some spiritual persons, however, remain in the childish ways of immature spirituality. These grown-up babes remain self-centred and egoistic.[13] Just like children, they continually seek to collect spiritual trophies. John calls this tendency spiritual childishness or like having a 'spiritual sweet tooth', which he considers as a hindrance to spiritual progress.[14]

Those who succeed in outgrowing spiritual childishness, experience a transformation in their attitudes and actions. Their childish self-centredness is superseded by a God-centredness and other-centredness. As John puts it:

> What I condemn is this possessiveness of heart... since everything else is imperfect attachment and possessiveness, any appetite for things must be uprooted if some degree of perfection is to be reached... Yet, until a soul is placed by God in the passive purgation of that dark night it cannot purify itself completely of these imperfections or others. But a person should, insofar as possible strive to do their part in purifying and perfecting themselves and thereby merit God's divine cure. In this cure God will heal them of what through their own efforts they were unable to remedy.[15]

Spiritual adulthood

In this stage, renunciation assumes its most intense form.
By following the path of *nada*, spiritual infants are
transformed into adults and mature spiritual persons. John
desires that his disciples forgo not merely the ordinary
pleasures of the world, but even those things that may be
called the luxuries of the spiritual life:

> this is the significance of following Christ and denying self, that
> the other method is perhaps a seeking of self in God – something
> entirely contrary to love. Seeking oneself in God is the same as
> looking for the caresses and consolations of God. Seeking God
> in oneself entails not only the desire to do without these
> consolations for God's sake, but also the inclination to choose
> for love of Christ all that is most distasteful whether in God or
> in the world; and this is what loving God means.[16]

As the person reaches spiritual adulthood, John's concern
is to help them to learn how to practise abandonment to
God's guidance and how to co-operate with his Spirit.
According to John, things both natural and supernatural
are useful to seekers only to the extent that they contribute
to their ascent to *nada*, the state of total detachment. If
they charm, occupy, and hold the person back, they are
hostile – and possible weapons in the hands of the world,
the flesh and the devil. Methods of meditation, cherished
notions, spiritual 'considerations' and so on are necessary
and they help the beginner, but they should be progressively
abandoned like ascending steps in a flight of stairs, because:

> none of the steps on a flight of stairs has any resemblance to the
> goal at the top towards which they are the means. If in climbing
> them we do not leave each one behind until there are no more,
> or if we want to stay on one of them, we would never reach the
> level and peaceful room at the top.[17]

Spiritual maturity

John believes that the ultimate reason for everything is love.[18] Love is both the way in which the person is united to God and the nature of the union itself. John personifies the person as a bride, who desires a more intense enkindling of love for the bridegroom, God. Love purifies the person for union with God. Even those whose love for God has been greatly increased by thinking about him and meditating on him, must learn to rest in love's quiet: "The proper advice for these individuals is that they must learn to abide in that quietude with a loving attentiveness to God and pay no heed to the imagination and its work."[19] Liberation will come by way of self-denial and mortification.[20] *Nada* is the central pillar of John's spiritual architecture, and the life of *nada* is the highest degree of humility.[21] The denudation proposed by John in the stage of spiritual maturity is absolute, but it is the passive aspect of this purification that plays the more significant role: in the passive nights God communicates "a general and obscure knowledge", "contemplation which is imparted through faith"[22]. Though the communication is not "delightful" but "painful"[23], its effect is to produce the "better love that stirs the person" to go out in search of the bridegroom. This love, in turn, assists and guides any asceticism, the active component of purification, that may be practised.

The 'natural path' of the imperfect spirit (seeking the goods of earth)

It is now time to turn to the broad path trodden by the imperfect spirits, placed on the right side of the 'path of *nada*'. Taking this path the imperfect spirit seeks after natural goods, the goods of earth. John lists the five attractions of this path: joy, knowledge, possessions, consolation and rest. Unfortunately, this path leads to a

dead end and gives the person less because more is sought.
The driving forces on this path are passions, desires and
appetites. John describes the effects of appetites on a person
as follows:

> the appetites are wearisome and tiring. They resemble children,
> restless and hard to please, always whining to their mother for
> this thing or that, and never satisfied... So is the soul wearied
> and tired by all its appetites and their fulfilment, because the
> fulfilment only causes more hunger and emptiness. An appetite,
> as they say, is like a fire that blazes up when wood is thrown on
> it, but it necessarily dies out when the wood is consumed.[24]

It is the joy the person hopes to find in possessions that
generates passions, desires and appetites. John speaks of six
kinds of objects or goods that can generate joy: temporal,
natural, sensory, moral, supernatural, and spiritual. He
defines joy as a delight of the will in an object esteemed
and considered fit, and further subdivides it into active and
passive varieties. The former is the result of understanding,
while the latter arises without any clear and distinct
understanding of the object of its joy, and is often the fruit
of God's action on the person. Whatever the origins of the
joy are, if the joy is possessive, then the appetites and
desires it generates always have the same negative
consequence. Besides being wearisome and tiring, the
appetites cause an even greater harm: they blind the person.
Like a moth attracted by the bonfire, the person walks
willingly towards their own perdition:

> The appetites blind and darken the soul because the appetites
> as such are blind... A moth is not helped much by its eyes
> because, blinded by its desire for the beauty of light, it will fly
> directly into a bonfire. Those who feed on their appetites are
> like a fish dazzled by a light that so darkens it that the fisherman's
> snares cannot be seen.[25]

By citing the example of prophet Samuel, who never
accepted any gifts from anyone to maintain his uprightness

(1 Sam 12:3), John points to the tendency of possessions to corrupt their owner and to the avarice that often follows the joy found in them.[26] The care for things other than God slowly makes the person feel lukewarm towards spiritual things and at a later stage makes them completely indifferent to God. The next stage in this decline is idolatry, that is, giving the place of honour to something other than God in our heart with a hope of deriving pleasure from it.[27] Spurred by the appetite and the desire for possession, some, as happened frequently in John's day, may even undertake extraordinary penances and exercises. John considers this as blindness due to ignorance:

> The ignorance of some is extremely lamentable; they burden themselves with extraordinary penances and many other exercises, thinking these are sufficient to attain union with divine wisdom. But such practices are insufficient if these souls do not diligently strive to deny their appetites... The appetites are like a cataract on the eyes or specks of dust in it; until removed they obstruct vision.[28]

John compares these victims of appetites to birds caught in birdlime. "A bird caught in birdlime has a twofold task: it must free itself and cleanse itself. And he who satisfies his appetite, suffers in a twofold way: he must detach himself and, after being detached, cleanse himself of what has clung to him."[29] While it is true that remaining in the initial stages for a considerable time provides a solid foundation for further progress on the path of perfection, some become stuck in them or even refuse to grow further because of the satisfaction they derive from their possessive childish ways. John discerns that imperfect spirits are still very much motivated by their natural desire to possess the goods of earth, even after saying farewell to their 'worldly life'.

Natural motivations that guide the imperfect spirit

John divides the goods of earth that are so much sought after by these imperfect spirits into three categories: temporal goods, natural goods and sensual goods.

Temporal goods are mainly of two kinds: they are wealth, social status, success at work and the like, on the one hand, and, children, family, marriage, friendship and the like on the other. None of these necessarily bring a person to sin, but human weakness can cause them to cling to any of these temporal goods and thus alienate themselves from God. The person must not rejoice in any of them, unless they help them to relate to God in a better way. Riches and marriage, for example, can become means of serving God better, but equally both can contribute to alienation from God.

Natural goods are beauty, grace, physical and spiritual qualities, right understanding, good reasoning, and so on. To rejoice in these for their own sake is vanity. The will must detach itself from the pleasures of natural blessings, paying them no heed, neither hoping for their increase nor grieving at their loss. Not to do so produces many evils derived from pride, and without these restraints the free enjoyment of natural blessings drags a person down to a sensual and coarse level, causing serious damage to the spiritual way in which they are trying to live their life.

Sensual goods are the pleasures of the exterior and interior bodily senses, that is, the pleasures of sight, hearing and smell, pleasures derived from touching and taste, pleasures deriving from the imagination and fantasy, and so on. To rejoice in these for their own sake is another form of vanity, presuming that the senses can bring one to God, who is beyond the senses. If we restrain our will from seeking after such pleasures, however, joy in sensual blessings can be good. By immediately leading the will to rise up to rejoice in God, we can leave the senses behind. But we must be cautious not to use prayer and devotion as a pretext for indulging our joy in sensual things. The spirit must be nourished and satisfied by the Spirit of God; only then will it lack nothing and desire nothing else.

John's image for those who maintain an appetite for the goods of earth is sharp and coarse – 'dogs'. The insatiable hunger for possessions binds a person to the things of the world and holds them back from enjoying the freedom of God's children:

> Those who go about feeding on creatures, then, are rightly designated as dogs and are deprived of the children's bread because they refuse to rise from the crumbs of creatures to the uncreated spirit of their Father. This is precisely why they wander about hungry as dogs. The crumbs serve more to whet their appetite than to satisfy their hunger... This is the characteristic of those with appetites; they are always dissatisfied and bitter, like someone who is hungry.[30]

Pitfalls in the natural path of the imperfect spirit

The imperfect spirits in the natural path exhibit two tendencies. Like the wife of Lot, they look back and wish to bring along with them at least some of their cherished possessions from the life they left behind. They afflict themselves with a yearning, like the people of Israel remembering the food they ate in Egypt (Num 11:4).[31] John says:

> so too, attachment to a creature defiles a soul, because this attachment makes it similar to the creature. Strokes of soot would ruin a perfect and extraordinarily beautiful portrait, so too inordinate appetites defile and dirty the soul, in itself, a perfect and extremely beautiful image of God.[32]

Even things done with an overtly pious motivation can become an abuse of the name of God. The complexity and diversity of human failure before God is amazing. Seeing the crafty ways of the devil, even in obviously religious activities, John exclaimed, "How many festivals, my God, do the children of this earth celebrate in your honour in which the devil has a greater role than you! And the devil, like a merchant, is pleased with these gatherings because he does more business on those days."[33] Traditionally all these failures have been classified as one or other of the seven cardinal or deadly vices, and John makes use of these categories in his explanations. Pride, envy and anger in particular, weaken the will in its love for God; all sins, in their many forms, undermine the spirit of detachment and darken the conscience, causing the person's spirit to fail. The end result is a loss of interest in spiritual exercises and withdrawal from God. We will now briefly look at how John understood the workings of each of the vices and the damage they can cause to a person on their path towards perfection.

Pride[34] is traditionally said to be the sin of Adam and Eve. In a sense all the other sins emerge from this one.[35] The desire to become like God led our first parents into disobedience. Pride is the inordinate self-love that seeks to make itself superior to all,[36] and refuses to accept reality. Pride would have all honour and happiness for itself alone. Vanities, arrogance, craving for superiority, curiosity, claiming to be indispensable and the like, are all the results of a proud mind and heart.[37] Pride makes people want God to will what they prefer, and they become sad if they have to follow God's will.[38]

Envy[39] is the child of pride and the twin of jealousy.[40] Envy is the product of the insecurity caused by the presence of pride. It bears grudges against others, produces intolerance, bigotry and prejudice. It desires self-exaltation and, if it fails, despises all and becomes despised by others. It takes unusual pleasure in defaming a neighbour's honour and destroying their peace and happiness. Envy is so despicable and subtle that it can attack even the most unsuspecting.

Anger,[41] the sibling of envy, is a destructive companion of pride. It feeds upon the resentment of envy until the violence inherent in envy breaks out into physical and emotional cruelty, psychological pain, rage, violence and even murder.[42] A vicious tongue, insulting, abusing, cursing and swearing with the aim of causing hurt are produced by anger, as are many other terrible combinations of hatred, including hatred at a social level which produces war, civil strife, class conflict, rebellion and factional spirit.[43]

Covetousness[44] or avarice is considered as a form of idolatry by Paul (Col 3:5).[45] It is a disordered desire that seeks to find in things a source of happiness.[46] This all-consuming vice constitutes a misuse of God's creation, accumulating material possessions in order to support our self-esteem and to provoke envy in our neighbours. It soon dissipates our love for God and turns it into a love for things, thus making an idol out of what God has given.[47]

Sloth,[48] the bosom companion of covetousness, is the failure of the will to work purposefully and constructively for God. It is a mean sin, which causes one to care less for others when there is no obvious and immediate personal gratification. A person infected with sloth is usually weary of the more spiritual sort of activities and flees from them since they are contrary to sensory satisfaction.[49]

Gluttony[50] is the sin that flows from a disordered 'animal' appetite. An obsession with sustenance constrains a person to the point of living to eat and drink. If it becomes an addiction, this pleasure blinds a person to such an extent that the intellect is incapacitated and rationality enters a deep slumber. Güided by instincts and drives, such a person leads an insignificant, self-centred life.[51]

Lust,[52] like gluttony, is the result of a disorderly animal appetite, through which a person becomes over-concerned with sensual satisfaction, so that their sensual desire demands a higher place in their life than their desire for God.[53] As such, it is a form of selfishness, which operates on the level of physical gratification to the detriment of all else, including the feelings and needs of others.

Consequences of the quest for the goods of earth

From the many examples given by John of the (harmful) consequences for those who attach themselves to visible objects while they search for God, who seek the goods of earth and rejoice in their possessions, we will consider four. First, absorption in this type of joy leads the person to stray off the road to union with God, producing a certain coarsening of the mind with regard to God and a clouding of their judgement. Secondly, it leads the will to wander off out of control, accepting, as John would say, greater liberty with regard to temporal things than is desirable. Thus the person gets so attached to temporal pleasures that they withdraw from the things of God and their Christian path. This results in many other imperfections, follies and vanities. Thirdly, this absorption and joy in the goods of earth sinks slowly to the level of immersion in disordered desires. It turns the whole will to covet worldly things, so that truth and justice are undermined and the will becomes weak, uncaring and lukewarm. The practice of their faith becomes a formality or a compulsion or continues out of habit, but there is no love in it. They have fallen away from God. Fourthly, evil completes its work by obliterating all attachment to God in the intellectual faculties – the understanding, the memory, and the will – (all three are explained briefly in the section 'John's Psychology' in the next chapter, page 120ff). Faith, hope and love leave the understanding, the memory and the will, and the person surrenders themselves into the hands of covetousness, forgetting all that God has ever meant to them. For such individuals, temporal blessings turn into idols, and if those goods are lost at this stage, their loss results in serious agitation, despair, emotional disturbance, and even suicide. As mentioned earlier, the most distressing fact of all is that the more the person seeks goods the less they get. John gives us the real reason behind this effect: "In so far as they possess things with attachment, they neither have nor possess anything. Rather, their heart is held by things and they suffer as a captive."[54]

Taking such joy in the possession of the goods of earth has certain direct effects; among others, John cites vanity of spirit, mental distraction, covetousness, indecency, interior and exterior agitation, impurity in thought, and envy. Joy in hearing causes distraction of the imagination, gossiping, envy, uncertain judgement and the wandering of thoughts. Joy in pleasant smells and fragrances causes aversion for the lowly, unsubmissiveness of heart in humble things, and spiritual insensitivity. Joy in food leads to gluttony, drunkenness, anger, discord, absence of charity towards one's neighbours and the poor, bodily disorders and lust. Joy in touch can leads to numerous kinds of harm, especially in sensual matters. Such joy also stimulates lust and makes one cowardly and timid. In order to avoid the displeasure of others, such individuals avoid all sorts of confrontation, while to attract attention and admiration they develop the habit of flattering.[55] John holds that our appetites harm us:

> Any appetite causes five kinds of harm in the soul: first, disquiet; second, turbidity; third, defilement; fourth, weakness; fifth, obscurity.[56] For the appetites weary, torment, darken, defile, and weaken the soul.[57]

John warns us of the great danger of detaching our love from God and attaching it to particular places, things, preachers and the like because of the benefit we have received through them.[58] Reliance upon such 'channels of grace' can only lead to partiality, inconstancy, dependence on place and person, indulging of the will in a type of devotion that gives us pleasure, and failure to renounce our own will for that of God. John does not deny the existence of special places of grace, but maintains that we must be inwardly detached from them and seek only to be in the darkness of faith, emptied in hope and dedicated to God in love. To aim for anything less than this lays us open to the danger of falling away from the desire to conform our will to God's will in the detachment of spirit which he asks of us.

John's description of the consequences of the inordinate passions for temporal things is practical and very much to the point. He makes it clear that the temporal goods in themselves are good; they should not be treated as necessary evils; it is human weakness that makes them impediments on the path towards God.[59]

The 'supernatural path' of the imperfect spirit (seeking the goods of heaven)

We will now turn to the broad path depicted on the left side of the 'perfect path', pursued by the imperfect spirits, who remain in the realm of spiritual infancy. We call this path 'supernatural' because those who follow this path, seek supernatural gifts or goods of heaven. Yet, the imperfections of the persons on this path are almost the same as the imperfections of those who follow the right-hand broad path of earthly goods. The only notable difference lies in the objects of their desire. While the former represents the pursuit of the goods of earth and the latter the goods of heaven, the desire for joy, knowledge, consolation and rest are essentially the same in both cases. Those seeking the goods of heaven are prey to all the seven cardinal vices, just as the seekers of the goods of earth are, except that the vices they are prone to are spiritual in nature, i.e. 'spiritual envy', 'spiritual anger', 'spiritual gluttony', and so on.

John holds that the goods of heaven are received by a person in two ways, bodily and spiritually.[60] Of the first type, the bodily goods of heaven, there are two kinds: one which is received through the exterior bodily senses and the other through the interior bodily senses. The second type, the spiritual goods of heaven, can be further categorised into two kinds: clear knowledge given to the spirit, without the aid of the bodily senses, such as visions, locutions, spiritual feelings and revelations; and an obscure and general type of knowledge, which is contemplation. John warns that those who attach importance to these experiences and feelings, are under the constant danger of losing their freedom. The source of such experiences may be good or bad, but attachment to such experiences is always bad and dangerous. Hence, says John, "The fly that clings to honey hinders its flight, and the soul that allows itself attachment to spiritual sweetness hinders its own liberty and contemplation."[61] We saw earlier that some imperfect spirits are still thoroughly motivated by their desire to possess the goods of earth; the same is true of other imperfect spirits in their desire for the goods of heaven.

Supernatural motivations that guide the imperfect spirit

The imperfect spirits on the spiritual path desire the goods of heaven not only because of the supernatural aura they possess, but because of the obvious benefits that they bring. John divides the goods of heaven into three kinds: moral goods, supernatural goods, and spiritual goods. If some of the categories John uses in discussions of this type seem a little strange to us at first, it is worth remembering that they belong to the religious language of his age but may correspond to our own experience if we pause to reflect (some we will understand easily, but not a few of the goods he describes are of an 'exalted' nature, and we may need to hang on tightly as John takes us past some dramatic experiences such as visions, 'locutions' and revelations which seem far beyond our own experience!).

Moral goods[62] include virtues like good habits, works of mercy, observance of the law, gentleness and politeness, social and political virtues, and all types of generally accepted forms of behaviour and practice which we feel proud of. Unlike the supernatural and spiritual goods whose description follows, moral goods contain some merit in themselves because of their intrinsic worth in bringing peace and tranquillity to human individuals and society. This being so, the intention of rejoicing in moral blessings must always be for the sake of honouring and serving God through them. Without this, all virtues are worthless in the sight of God.

Supernatural goods[63] are free gifts received by a person without any special merit on the part of the recipient. The gifts discussed by Paul in the First Letter to the Corinthians,[64] like the power to heal, ability to do miracles, the gift of prophesy, power of interpretation, the gift of tongues, discernment of spirits, wisdom and faith, are all classified by John as supernatural goods. Bodily supernatural gifts are received through the heightening of the five senses of the body beyond their natural ability, resulting in certain effects: the sense of sight may produce visions of saints, of angels, or of other apparitions from heaven or hell, bright lights and so on; through the sense of hearing the person may receive messages, or hear words spoken without seeing whoever it is who utters them. Through the sense of touch the person may experience delightful physical sensations; or through the senses of smell and taste may become conscious of pleasant perfumes or flavours.[65]

The next form of supernatural knowledge is that received by what John called interior bodily senses – imagination and fantasy (this new pair of 'interior senses' is briefly explained in the section 'John's Psychology' in the next chapter, page 120ff). Grace as well as 'demonic' influences work upon these interior senses to produce the supernatural equivalent of meditation. This means that supernatural knowledge now enters the intellect, not through actively thinking about aspects of our faith as we do in meditation, but passively through the direct intervention of the supernatural. This supernatural imaginary knowledge is beyond the natural powers of the interior senses, even though it uses the same sort of exterior sense material as the imagination does when acting naturally. John maintains that the sort of knowledge referred here includes certain events reported in Scripture, such as Isaiah's vision of God in glory in the temple, the many visions in the book of Daniel, the dreams of Pilate's wife, and the transfiguration of Christ. The effects are, in principle, the same as those produced by meditation but, because the visions are supernatural in origin, their effects are, in fact, more powerful and have a greater influence on us. Likewise, because they are more interior and happen deeper within us than external supernatural visions, they make a far deeper impression.

Another type of supernatural knowledge enters the understanding directly, without the use of the senses, through visions, locutions, spiritual feelings and revelations. Visions are communications in which the person appears to see something, although nothing is actually seen by the physical sense of sight. In locutions the person appears to hear something, although nothing is physically heard. Spiritual feelings include the experience of smelling, tasting and touching, although nothing is actually experienced by those senses. *Visions* received in this way often correspond to the results of meditation produced by the imagination working with the understanding, but in this case both imagination and understanding are in the dark and no meditation actually occurs. John identifies three types of *locutions*: successive, formal and substantial. Successive locutions are teachings about aspects of the Christian faith. Formal locutions could be on any subject. Substantial differ from formal locutions only in that they leave a more powerful impression on the soul. *Spiritual feelings* are of two types. One concerns the affections of the will and the other moves deep in the 'substance' of the soul. *Revelations*, associated with the spirit of prophecy, are of two sorts. The first sort gives the intellectual knowledge of the truths of God, with regard to God himself and in relation to his creation. This illumination may occur concerning the attributes of God, for example, his goodness, omnipotence, graciousness and so on, or concerning his action in the world, for example, prophecy and discernment. The second sort discloses the hidden secrets regarding the mystery of God and his works, revealed through prophecies concerning the future and through the interpretation of past events.

Spiritual goods[66] are those gifts of God which are given to an individual person and concern them and their relationship with God alone; they motivate a person in spiritual matters and prepare them for communication with God. This means, of course, that such gifts are not intended to have an immediate role to play in the lives of other believers. This type of gift consists of two distinct forms of communication from God: one is delightful and the other, occurring during the passive night of the spirit, is painful. Each can be received in two ways: in a clear and distinct manner that can be understood, or in a dark and confused form. Spiritual goods are received in different ways by each of the spiritual faculties: spiritual goods of knowledge are 'enjoyed' in the faculty of understanding, those goods which affect the imagination are enjoyed in the memory, and those which move our affections in the will.

John expresses his concern about the seeking of supernatural benefits and communications in very strong words, "I fail to see how a person who tries to get knowledge in this supernatural way – as well as the one who commands this or gives consent – can help but sin, at least venially, no matter how excellent the motives or how advanced in perfection that person may be."[67]

Pitfalls in the supernatural path of the imperfect spirit

For Teresa of Jesus, the mother of the Carmelite reform, the devil was forever eroding the spirit of prayer, the resolve and so on, of those who journey to God, working away like a "noiseless file".[68] John, too, knew that in the realm of the supernatural this 'enemy of our salvation' is as able as anywhere else to bring the person to ruin, producing in this case all the delights the exterior and interior senses could desire. A direct intervention from the devil, through the gateway of imagination or fantasy with a consent on the part of the person could destroy all progress towards spiritual nakedness. A possessive entertaining of supernatural sensual delights could easily make a person think they were of particular and unique importance in the eyes of God. John clearly saw that we should not grasp or hold onto supernatural goods for exactly the same reasons as we should not grasp or hold onto natural or earthly goods. Even what comes from God may lead us to deceive ourselves.[69] All supernatural goods must be rejected as means for reaching God not only because they are limited (unlike the God who may have given them) and thus cannot carry their recipient all the way to the infinite God,[70] but also because they enkindle and strengthen the seven capital vices. Let us now see what John has to say about each of the seven capital vices in their new supernatural attire.

Spiritual pride[71] makes people self-satisfied with their works and with themselves. They condemn others in thought when they notice that they do not have the kind of devotion they themselves desire to have. Some reach such a degree of pride that they fail to find anybody good but themselves, they even condemn others in deed and word, and slander them, thus seeing the speck in their brother's eye and overlooking the log in their own (Mt 7:3).[72] They love to be praised by others, and sometimes they even seek such praise, but have a real dislike of praising others. Religious may blame their superior, anyone can blame a confessor, when these do not approve of their behaviour or attitude, and consequently change confessors to suit their taste. In order to impress their confessor, they do not make a frank and humble confession of their sins and faults with all their ulterior motives, which are usually petty, mean and uncharitable. Wishing to be esteemed as very spiritual and devout, John says, they plan circumstances that are calculated to show themselves off to the best advantage, such as assuming certain postures, ways of speaking, sighs, and "well-timed ecstasies!"[73] Some beginners overlook faults in themselves they should be very quick to notice; at other times, they are over-depressed by their faults since they think themselves already worthy of the halo. As a result, they become angry and impatient with themselves.

Spiritual envy[74] is felt by imperfect spirits who experience real annoyance when they notice the spiritual progress of others and feel grief at being outdone in virtue.[75] This, in turn, leads them to criticise others when they are praised for their virtue. And when others fail to praise them, they are very disappointed because this is what they seek. They also desire to be preferred above others.[76]

Spiritual anger[77] can be directed against the defects of others, or against the person's own imperfections. When 'supernatural goods maniacs' are deprived of spiritual consolations, they experience a sense of frustration. Some are so irritated by the deprivation of consolations that the smallest things upset them, and this can reach such a pass that no one is able put up with them any longer. John goes on to speak of another form of spiritual anger, whereby such people exercise an unholy zeal towards others, criticising them angrily in their thoughts, and at times in words, and setting themselves up as 'masters of virtue' and a norm for others.[78] At other times, they are so impatient with themselves on account of their own imperfections that they would wish to see themselves become saints overnight. They resolve much, and promise a great deal, but as they are not humble and do not sufficiently distrust themselves, they strain and expect much while they accomplish little. This is so because they do not have the patience to wait for the necessary help that God will give according to his plan.[79]

Spiritual covetousness[80] or avarice develops due to the desire to outdo others. In the process, John noted, some weaken themselves by fasting and kill themselves with penance; some even dare to perform these penances contrary to obedience.[81] Those who succumb to this vice are disappointed and become very impatient when they do not find the consolation they seek in spiritual exercises. They spend all their time listening to spiritual conversations, acquiring and reading many spiritual books which treat of spiritual consolations, instead of cultivating a spirit of mortification and detachment. They become walking piety stores, loaded with pictures, medals, rosaries, chaplets, crosses and relics. They insist that these objects must be made of special materials and according to a certain style. Here, it is not devotion that attracts them, but the workmanship and variety of religious articles.

Spiritual sloth[82] manifests itself in the flight from spiritual practices which do not bring sensible pleasure and sweetness. Thus, the imperfect spirits who have fallen into this vice practise prayer with indifference and are irregular in keeping the time set aside for it, because it frequently fails to bring them the satisfaction they seek. Consequently, they desert the road to perfection, which demands the surrender of their own will to God's will. Such people measure God by themselves, and find it repugnant to conform their will to God's will. Being attached to sweetness and consolation, they lack in the fortitude needed to bear the trials of perfection. Instead, they run away from everything that is hard, and take offence at the cross, the true source of the delights of the spirit.

Spiritual gluttony[83] can take various shapes and forms. The imperfect spirits who are prey to this vice find the motivation for all their spiritual practices in the satisfaction and delight they derive from them. They think that gratifying and satisfying themselves is the same as serving God and satisfying him.[84] In their spiritual exercises they are drawn more by the desire for spiritual sweetness than by detachment and discretion. This leads them to exceed the moderation that should govern the practice of virtues. So they kill themselves or shorten their lives with penances and severe fasts. Religious may fail to act in accordance with obedience, and, in some cases, act contrary to obedience. Setting bodily penance above the true penance of the will, such people perversely have little desire to perform the penances that obedience obliges them to perform, so attached are they to their own will. Often they use subtle means to obtain what they desire from their spiritual masters. Others, when they attempt to relate with God, strive with all their might and zeal to produce some sensible sweetness and pleasure, and if they fail, think that they have accomplished nothing. This reveals their low concept of God based, to a great extent, on the senses: they wish to feel and taste God as though they could understand him and reach him by their own efforts. The same is true of their mental prayer, which they think consists in experiencing sensible pleasure and devotion, and they strive to obtain this by great effort, wearying and fatiguing their faculties and their heads. In the end, they fail to persevere in this most important exercise, for they practise it more from inclination and feeling, than a desire for real progress in virtue and union with God. Such people, being so attached to consolations and sweetness, are reluctant to practise mortification and detachment in sober earnestness.

Spiritual lust.[85] John considers not only actual sins against purity or chastity as instances of spiritual lust, but every imperfection including 'impure acts and feelings'. These experiences are often those which a person does not desire to have and are beyond their power to prevent, often occurring when a person is deeply recollected in prayer, or is receiving the Sacrament of Reconciliation or Communion. The first cause of this experience lies in the fact that the body also shares in the spiritual pleasures and the delights of the soul, but in a way which accords with its own nature. Thus spiritual joy overflowing into the body is experienced by the body in a pleasure that may be called sensual or even sexual. This occurs not only in beginners, but also in those who have made progress. This imperfection is checked when the sensual part is renewed in the purgation of the dark night, or the passive trial, of the senses. A second cause of these weaknesses is the devil himself, who tries by the use of such imaginations and feelings to persuade the beginner to give up their spiritual exercises, leading them to think that their devout practice is the cause of the impurity they are suffering from. By means of such thoughts the devil tries to throw the individual into a state of panic, which causes them to give up their efforts to achieve the much-desired union with God. The third cause is the fear itself created by the presence of these feelings and images in a person's mind during spiritual exercises or prayer. John speaks furthermore of certain spiritual friendships which are founded more on a hidden or unacknowledged sexual attraction than on a real desire for spiritual betterment and love of God. When this is the case, the love of God diminishes, sensual love grows and brings remorse of conscience. In passive trials, love of God will be strengthened and purified, and sensual love will be brought under control.

Consequences of the quest for the goods of heaven

As we have noted earlier, those who rejoice in the possession of supernatural goods are vulnerable to deception and are easy victims of the evil spirit. John says, using the language of his time and reflecting on the pressing concerns of his time, that the devil then induces many into believing vain visions and false prophecies, striving to make them presume that God and the saints speak to them. Frequently, John says, they believe their fantasy. They become filled with presumption and pride and, drawn by vanity and arrogance, they allow themselves to be seen in exterior acts of apparent holiness, such as raptures and other exhibitions. They become rather too bold and lose the holy fear of God, which is the key and guardian of all virtues.[86] Some of these unfortunate individuals may even become sidetracked, in order to satisfy their ambition. They attempt to use God to achieve their own ends and endanger their own faith by putting it to the test in worthless matters.[87] This is the warning John has for those who wish to possess the goods of heaven:

> A soul should never dare to want to accept these communications, even though, as I say, they are from God. If it does, six kinds of harm will result. First, faith will gradually diminish, for sensible

experiences greatly detract from it... Second, if left unrejected
these sensory things are an impediment to the spirit because they
detain the soul and prevent the spirit from soaring to the
invisible... Third, the soul begins to develop a possessive attitude
towards these communications and fails to continue on its
journey to genuine renunciation and nakedness of spirit. Fourth,
individuals gradually lose the effect of these communications
and the interior spirituality they produce because the individuals
set their eyes on the sensible aspect... Fifth, individuals gradually
lose God's favours because they receive these favours as something
belonging to themselves and do not profit well by them... Sixth,
in desiring to accept them one opens the door to the devil. The
devil can then deceive one by other communications, expertly
feigned and disguised as genuine.[88]

The person should not, therefore, endanger any progress
already made by seeking to possess whatever is presented to
the understanding in a supernatural way: all such experiences
must be rejected as inadequate means to bring us to the
union with God. Faith alone is capable of uniting us to
God.[89] Another reason for this rejection, says John, is that
the supernatural gifts may be exercised by people not in a
state of grace or charity, as the biblical examples of Balaam,
Solomon, and Simon Magus show.[90] Recipients of these
gifts should not rejoice in them because of any temporal
benefits they bring. They should rejoice when they reap
the spiritual benefit these gifts confer, which is serving
God and loving him through the supernatural blessings he
gives. Desire to do the will of God alone is the condition
required of the will if it is called to use these gifts with
safety. John cautions:

Furthermore, the desire for such locutions and attachment to
them will cause these persons to answer themselves and think
that God is responding and speaking to them... I say, therefore,
that these locutions can be a serious obstacle to souls in their
journey towards divine union because by paying attention to
them souls are drawn far from the abyss of faith. The intellect
should remain in obscurity and journey by love in darkness of
faith and not by much reasoning.[91]

For those who rejoice in the possession of moral goods, seven kinds of spiritual harm await. The first consists of vanity, pride, vainglory, presumption and boasting, which come about because the person esteems their own good works. The second is the tendency of the person to judge others' good works as inferior to their own. The third harm is that the person is very much inclined only to do things that bring them gratification and praise. The fourth harm derives from the fact that because their good deeds have an ulterior motive, such persons turn them into vehicles of self-promotion, and adore themselves more than God. The failure to advance in the path of perfection because the person finds the difficulty involved distasteful, is the fifth harm. The sixth is the mistaken belief that works which give greater satisfaction are actually better than those which do not, while in fact difficult and unpleasant things could be just what the person needs for their progress. The seventh harm which comes from a possessive enjoyment of moral goods is that the person becomes so attached to the pleasure they find in them that they can no longer listen to advice or reasonable instructions about the sort of work they ought to do.[92]

Self-esteem and pride lead one to develop a sort of contempt for those who lag behind and a jealousy towards those who are more advanced. John even challenges the genuineness of those spiritual directors and confessors, who are carried away by the revelations and manifestations revealed to them by their clients.[93]

Path of the perfect spirit

'Night' is the image John uses to symbolise the spiritual experience of a person journeying along the path of *nada*. The image of night conspicuous advantages: unlike 'ascent', night cannot be organised into a spiritual programme; it demands passivity more than effort; it limits activity, hides objects, increases danger, and transforms everything into strange, frightening silhouettes. Yet, at the same time, the night protects and helps those who hide from their enemies. The dark night experience functions in two ways: one is negative and the other positive. Negative because the night hides everything; a person feels incapable of working; God is hidden; prayer becomes tasteless; life has no meaning. Positive, because, thanks to this aridity and darkness, the person can finally become free from so many of its enemies like egotistical scheming, demands, attachments, pastimes, curiosity, and so on, that habitually hinder them in times of spiritual well-being.[94]

But as we said, being in the night and encountering *nada* is not a delightful experience. All the faculties of the person, both internal and external, rise up to revolt against their impending annihilation. Entry into night means that the faculties of reason and sense-perception are no longer able to help, and this throws the person into total helplessness and confusion. These faculties warn the person of the great risk involved in depending on faith alone. They caution the individual of the possible danger in following an uncertain course, blinded by love, with a hope that has no certainty, except trust in the mercy of God. There is, however, no alternative path towards God other than this path of 'dark faith'. John teaches, "Since God is inaccessible, be careful not to concern yourself with all that your faculties can comprehend and your senses feel, so that you do not become satisfied with less and lose the lightness of soul suitable for going to him."[95] Darkness, fear, temptations, doubt, feeling of helplessness, and so on, are in fact part and parcel of the path of *nada*:

> The trials that those who are to reach this state suffer are threefold: trials, discomforts, fears, and temptations from the world; and these in many ways: temptations, aridities and afflictions in the senses; and tribulations, darkness, distress, abandonment, temptations, and other trials in the spirit. In this way a soul is purified in its sensory and spiritual parts.[96]

The only comfort a person walking in *nada* can have is prayer. John divides prayer into two basic types: meditative prayer and contemplative prayer. Meditative prayer is performed through the use of the sensory faculties, which include both the five external senses and the imagination and fantasy, and the spiritual faculties, which consist of the person's intellect, memory and will. Because of the significant role of the senses and personal effort to form and reflect upon images or thoughts required by meditation, John speaks of meditation as a work of the senses. Reflection upon an image or thought that they have formed enables the individual to draw some knowledge and love of God out of meditation. This knowledge and love are the primary purposes of meditation. Meditation serves another purpose as well: the individual develops a habit and delight in relating to God rather than to the profane.

Contemplation demands a drastic change in the method of prayer that is used – silence and the cessation of the activity of both sensory and spiritual faculties.[97] This new method requires the application of *nada* to everything that was comfortable and desirable in the previous stage. Anything that is not God is denied in this process.[98] Even the interventions of God and the gifts coming from him are placed in the consuming fire of *nada*. The person no longer feels a desire to receive anything either from God or from the world, because, the receiver – the self – is negated and is not operating. John explains:

> Let there be no particular knowledge or affection or other consideration in any of the spiritual faculties (memory, intellect and will); and let there be no other digressions, forms, images, or figures of objects, or other natural operations in any of the bodily senses and faculties, either interior or exterior (the imagination, phantasy; sight, hearing, and so on).[99]... The soul that journeys to God, but does not shake off its cares and quiet its appetites, is like one who drags a cart uphill.[100]... If you wish to attain holy recollection, you will do so not by receiving but by denying.[101]... Souls will be unable to reach perfection who

do not strive to be content with having nothing, in such fashion that their natural and spiritual desire is satisfied with emptiness; for this is necessary in order to reach the highest tranquillity and peace of spirit.[102]... All things are nothing to it, and it is nothing in its own eyes; God alone is its all.[103]

This "mortification of the desires and denial of pleasures in all things"[104] is not meant to make the person insensible, but rather to liberate them from the dark prison of self-centred gratification and give freedom to choose the true good.[105] For the person's own part, these hazards are an adventure of love, rather than a burden forced upon them.[106] Those who manage to reach the end of the night of the senses, become integrated persons sharply focussed on God. In John's view, God is the source of human contentment,[107] not only eternally but also in this life. Eternally, we can be united with God in the beatific vision; in this life, we can be united with God through the theological virtues of faith in the intellect, hope in the memory, and charity in the will.

Motivation that guides the perfect spirit

We have noted that there is no place for appetites or selfish motivations on the path of *nada*. The only driving force that sustains the life of the pilgrim on their path is love. Ascetical practices and the denial of material objects are all aimed at enhancing love. The person, in turn, is only motivated by the hope of enhancing the glory of God:

> If you desire that devotion be born in your spirit and that the love of God and the desire for divine things increase, cleanse your soul of every desire, attachment, and ambition in such a way that you have no concern about anything.[108]... Endeavour always that things be not for you, nor you for them, but forgetful of all, abide in recollection with your Bridegroom.[109]

It is the experience of God's love that ignites the fire of love within the person. We love because God loved us first (1 Jn 4:19). Since the natural tendency of the self is to seek to do its own will, to surrender to the will of God causes suffering. However, when filled with the love of God the person prefers 'suffering' through the surrendering of the self-will to the enjoyment that entails the rejection of God's will. Here we need to stop a minute and examine what John means by suffering. A person who suffers because of love, in fact, is suffering only in a very superficial sense. The internal satisfaction and joy that a person obtains, even at the very moment of suffering, far exceeds the pain they bear. For example, the pain a woman suffers in giving birth to her child is borne more easily because of the end in view, the child she had wanted, who is the fruition of her love.[110] Because the person loves God so deeply they become bound to the will of God:

> God must be served because of who he is and other motives must not be intermingled with this one. Not serving God only because of who he is, is the same as serving God without having God as the final cause.[111]... Habitual voluntary imperfections that are never completely overcome not only hinder the divine union, but also the attainment of perfection. Such imperfections are: the habit of being very talkative, a small unconquered attachment, such as to a person, to clothing, to a cell, a book, or to the way food is prepared, and to other conversations and little satisfactions in tasting things, in knowing, and hearing, and the like.[112]... Be interiorly detached from all things and do not seek pleasure in any temporal things, and your soul will concentrate on goods you do not know.[113]... Let Christ Crucified be enough for you, and with him suffer and take your rest, and hence annihilate yourself in all inward and outward things.[114]... Whoever knows how to die in all will have life in all.[115]

Though the glory of God becomes the motivating factor behind every action of the person on the path of *nada,* it does not agitate them or lead them to hold an aggressive attitude like 'glory of God by any means'. There is great peace in the heart of the one who remains in *nada*, because they are guided not by their own will but that of God, directed by the Spirit of God:

> Take neither great nor little notice of who is with you or against you, and try always to please God. Ask him that his will be done in you. Love him intensely, as he deserves to be loved.[116]... Detachment from exterior things, dispossessed of interior things, disappropriated of the things of God – neither will prosperity detain you nor adversity hinder you.[117]... Strive to preserve your heart in peace; let no event of this world disturb it; reflect that all must come to an end.[118]

Milestones on the path of the perfect spirit

The perfect path of *nada*, difficult as it is, provides its own benefits and even what we might term compensations, all of which assist the person in their attempt to attain total nakedness of the spirit. The benefits are in fact certain virtues which John opposes to the seven cardinal vices we have already considered. John places all nine of them on his sketch of the Mount Carmel.

Peace[119] is the result of different virtues, especially meekness and humility. Meekness is the gentlest of the virtues, which does not mean to say that a meek person has to be feeble or weak-kneed, because to remain meek actually requires extraordinary strength. A meek person needs the strength to absorb the anger of others and not to return blow for blow, the courage to withstand humiliation and the self-control to promote harmony out of conflict. Meekness means standing firm for God and for peace. Humility is the attitude of being honest and realistic about ourselves, and as the opposite of pride requires that we be not blinded to our own faults or to the virtues of others by our self-esteem. Humility recognises that we are not God, but dependent on God for all graces, even life itself, and therefore we need him and need others.[120]

John presents humility as one of the virtues that irritates the devil most, and as a sure protection against his traps.[121] This virtue deepens as one progresses on the path of *nada*. Humility is not about self-depreciation and the hiding of God-given talents in public while inwardly basking in self-admiration.[122] Humility is accepting the truth, it is the first fruit of love and light.[123] The perception that we are 'nothing' and our work is 'nothing' should spring from a clear self-understanding, a perfect love and clear knowledge of God. Such a perception is the result of the light which permits us to have a glimpse of what God is and what we are in comparison. Humility also involves proclaiming the favours received from God and using our talents for the benefit of those around us and for the greater glory of God (Lk 17:10). The spirit of humility, according to John, contains no vanity, no ostentation, nothing unattractive. It is filled with sincerity and spreads abroad the fire of charity.[124]

Joy.[125] Negation and self-discipline, practised by means of renunciation and detachment, automatically generate an inner joy, which is beyond the realm of bodily pleasures. This occurs because of the right use of the God-given freedom. A preference of the will of God to the attractions of creatures saves the person from all the miseries which result from wrong choices. The absence of material riches is soon substituted by an inner contentment; the absence of possessions is substituted by a liberating openness.

Happiness[126] is an attitude or an inclination of the heart, but the person who manages to disentangle themselves from enslaving attachments to creatures and sets their heart wholly on God experiences certain positive effects in the body too. The freedom obtained as a result of detachment removes the fear of losing the coveted objects, and in the absence of fear and threat, the body remains relaxed and buoyant. Just as a bird, set free from the thread that bound it to the ground, takes to flight, the person feels a great sense of relief as they enter the experience of *nada.* This happiness is directly proportional to the intensity of the attachment and the pain it caused due to the fear of losing it.

Delight[127] is the elation of soul which comes about as a result of the freedom obtained from the oppressive burdens of the innumerable desires. The new-found closeness to God which results from the detachment and renunciation of the profane generates in the person a delight that is different from the inner joy and external happiness previously experienced. Detachment is an interior disposition, while renunciation refers more to exterior acts. Detachment means the *affective* denial of inordinate desires and pleasures in creatures, while renunciation implies an *effective* denial and an actual turning from such desires and pleasures. Detachment is absolute while renunciation is relative. Together they allow the person to experience life as coming directly from God. A person in this state may exclaim with Paul, "I live, now not I, but Christ lives in me" (Gal 2:20).[128]

Wisdom.[129] Another beneficial effect of walking in *nada* is the light of a wisdom that shines on the wayfarer. This heavenly light, which eclipses the light of human reason, enables the person to "go from all to all by denying all in all".[130] However, this denial is not absolute and immediate. It is progressive and relative until one reaches the end of the journey, where the self-surrender reaches its culmination. Such wisdom enables the person to determine prudently the degree of detachment required in each stage of growth in the life of *nada.* At the moment of death, if a person is able to make an absolute renunciation of all creatures out of love for God, then they can make a perfect choice of God in charity, and in the moment of death, the paschal mystery with its double aspect of emptiness and fullness (*kenosis* and *pleroma*) shines forth in them.

Justice[131] is a state in which everything gets its due. The capacity to act or judge with justice is a grace from God. When Jesus told the Pharisees to give Caesar what belongs to Caesar and to God what belongs to God (Lk 20:25), he demonstrated the rule of justice. Even on the path of *nada*, the path of absolute negation, the person has to follow this rule. Nothing that God has created is worthless. The Bible testifies that God viewed his creation, found that it was good and was satisfied (Gen 1:25). Each creature has a role to play in God's plan to make us his children, to 'deify' us, and ignorance of this fact leads to the abuse and depreciation of creation. John knew that strong measures were often needed to establish order and to eradicate certain deep-rooted inordinate attachments to created things, but this should in no way lead us to mistreat any person or creature, and he strongly cautions his readers against any harmful treatment of the body for the sake of spiritual advancement.

Fortitude[132] is the path by which the selfish laziness of the will is overcome through persistence in goodwill to others and acts of love to God. Perseverance is the willingness and effort to remain aware of others and open-hearted towards them, even, and especially, when there is nothing to be gained for the self.

Charity[133] grows in proportion to the freedom the person has from all that is contrary to it. Charity reduces envy and helps the person to grow in self-sacrifice and self-giving dedication to what is good, as well as giving capacity to work for the benefit and the welfare of others. Charity, being generous, continues to 'give and does not count the cost'. Love of neighbour and of God shows itself in the stewardship of the resources possessed by the person, who turns any material benefits they may possess into a means of blessing for others and an expression of dedication to God. As John remarks of such people, "their pleasure is to know how to live for love of God and of neighbour".[134]

Piety.[135] There is a close relationship between progress in *nada* and the development of true piety. *Nada* consciousness produces in the individual an intense longing for God. John speaks of it as "love's urgent longings",[136] which enables the person to undertake the tedious journey through the dark night of *nada*. The suffering as a result of the absence of external or internal support leads the person to place all their hope in God and strengthens them to persevere in the process of self-renewal. However, once active purification is achieved, these urgent longings of love cease. John explains the reasons:

> To enter the night of the senses and denude itself of the sensible things, the soul needed the longings of sensible love.[137] ... since the strength and efficacy of the dark fire of love that assails it is communicated and impressed on it passively, the darkness, strength and warmth of love cease when the assault terminates.[138]

What the path of *nada* 'achieves'

The advantages of following the path of *nada* are many. In so far as the person is purged of their sensory appetites and *afflictions*, they obtain freedom of spirit in which they acquire the twelve fruits of the Holy Spirit.[139] They also find a remarkable liberation from the hands of their enemies: the world, the flesh, and the devil. For when sensory delight and gratification in created things are quenched, neither the world, nor sensuality, nor the devil has any power against the spirit.[140] The person feels themselves totally transformed. As John puts it, "When God grants this supernatural favour to the soul, so great a union is caused that all the things of both God and the soul become one in participant transformation, and the soul appears to be God more than a soul. Indeed, it is God by participation."[141] Although in this stage the person is saturated with all kinds of virtues, the most conspicuous virtues they possess, according to John, are peace, meekness, and strength:

> this bed is in flower, made from the flowers of virtues, and all these virtues are peaceful, meek, and strong, the bed itself is built up in peace; and the soul peaceful, meek, and strong. These are three properties against which no war can be waged, neither by the world nor the devil nor the flesh. [142]

When the appetites and 'concupiscence' (the traditional word for our congenital inclination to sin) are tamed by following the path of *nada*, the person dwells in spiritual peace and tranquillity. Where neither the appetites nor concupiscence command, there can be no disturbance, only God's peace and consolation.[143] The person carries about with them a habitual remembrance of God. In the patient forbearance of these aridities and emptiness, and through perseverance in their spiritual exercises without consolation or satisfaction, the person practises the love of God, since they are no longer motivated by any gratification they find in their work, but only by God. The four main benefits of remaining in this night are: peace, habitual remembrance of God, cleanness and purity of soul, and the practice of virtue.[144]

The benefits derived from following the path of *nada*, include the development of a generosity which eliminates covetousness, freedom of action in the soul, clarity of reason, rest and tranquillity, peaceful confidence in God growing out of a will committed in love to the reverence and worship of God. The benefits of detachment from sensual blessings include the preservation of virtue and the strength of spirit; the transformation of what is sensual into the spiritual and that of the animal into the rational; improved judgement, even of the deep things of God; and an actual increased benefit derived from temporal things because they are no longer a threat to the detached will. In fact, detachment from temporal blessings leads to a greater ability to enjoy them because the person can now do so without the anxieties caused by attachment to them. The person rejoices in such good things with a clear sense of their true worth, because they neither possess them nor are possessed by them. Finally, detachment leaves the will free for God. When everything unlike and unconformed to God is cast out because of the love for him and the will that operates in the person becomes nothing other than God's will, the person is transformed into God:

> Consequently, a soul must strip itself of everything pertaining to creatures and of its actions and abilities (of its understanding, satisfaction, and feeling), so that when everything unlike and unconformed to God is cast out, it may receive the likeness of God. And the soul will receive this likeness because nothing contrary to the will of God will be left in it. Thus, it will be transformed in God.[145]

Conclusion

Our spiritual pilgrimage, which commences with an attitude of detachment and departure from the 'ways of the world' and its attractions, seems at first glance to offer us a number of paths that all lead to the same eternal destination. This is not John's opinion. For John, there are no choices other than the *kenotic* path of *nada*, which Jesus has indicated to us and walked himself. Using the 'Redesigned Sketch of Mount Carmel' as a basis, we have analysed the path of *nada*, outlining the four stages of spiritual growth and the three paths trodden by persons in their pursuit of God. We have observed how John presents the path of *nada* as the perfect path that leads to the ultimate human destination, God, and how all other paths are unable to conduct the wayfarer to their goal. Moving along the path of *nada*, the individual can outgrow spiritual childishness and move towards spiritual maturity. This journey, however, is a joint venture undertaken by God and the traveller. From the human side, co-operation with God's grace requires an act of surrender rather than of self-assertion. The path of *nada*, and the freedom it generates, have the ability to recreate the original harmony which was lost as a result of human greed and possessiveness: this path and no other, because the bird held even with a thread remains trapped until the thread is severed.[146]

Spiritual infants have to realise that the value of good works is not based on their number or quality, but on the love for God which inspires them. If a person's love for God is not enkindled by those good works and if those acquired goods fail to lead the person to *nada* or nakedness of spirit, they should be regarded as impediments on the path towards perfection. The person must not allow their good works and moral and material goods to distract them from God, and they must not become attached to all the pleasures, consolations and other benefits derived from them. The person should desire that God alone rejoice in their good works, and should be content to do them without becoming attached to them, because attachments will increase vanity and self-love, resulting in a lack of progress along the road to perfection and a loss of God's favour. In contrast, the benefits of detachment include freedom from demonic deception, a greater facility in good works, the ability to judge any matter in hand more clearly, poverty of spirit, meekness, humility, freedom from the seven capital vices, and so on. Detachment from joy in moral blessings gives the person the security to do good works with confidence, because the works are done for the glory of God alone. John holds that a total detachment or a descent to nothingness is an ascent to God.[147] The following chapter will focus on the progressive steps suggested by John to reach this ultimate nothingness.

NOTES

1 *A* Prologue, 2-3
2 O. Rodriguez, *Saint John of the Cross*, 39-46.
3 *1A* 13,10.
4 For the original 'Sketch of Mount Carmel' drafted by John of the Cross and the English translation of the terms used in John's original drawing see pages 14 and 15.
5 For the 'Redesigned Sketch of Mount Carmel' see page 16.
6 *1N* 11,1.
7 *1N* 1,1-3.
8 *2N* 11,2.
9 *2A* 24,9.
10 *2A* 15,2.
11 *1A* 14,2.
12 *LF* 3,66.
13 *1N* 7,3.
14 *1N* 6,6.
15 *1N* 3,1.
16 *2A* 7,5.
17 *2A* 12,5
18 *C* 38,5.
19 *2A* 12,8.
20 E.E. Larkin, "The Dark Night of John of the Cross", *The Way* 14 (1974), 14
21 *2A* 7,11.
22 *2A* 11,4.
23 *3A* 33,3-5.
24 *1A* 6,6.
25 *1A* 8,3.
26 *3A* 19,4.
27 *3A* 19,5-8.
28 *1A* 8,4.
29 *Sayings*, 22.
30 *1A* 6,3.
31 *1A* 5,3.
32 *1A* 9,1.
33 *3A* 38,3.
34 *1N* 2,1-8.
35 B. Dent, *My Only Friend is Darkness: Living the Night of Faith with St John of the Cross* (Trivandrum: Carmel Publishing Centre, 1996), 36-38.
36 L. of St Joseph, *The Secret of Sanctity*, 96.
37 T. Spidlík, *The Spirituality of the Christian East*, Christian Study Series -79 (Michigan: Cistercian Publications, 1986), 254.
38 *1N* 7,3.
39 *1N* 7,1.

40 L. of St Joseph, *The Secret of Sanctity*, 97.
41 *1N* 5,1-3.
42 B. Dent, *My Only Friend*, 41.
43 T. Spidlík, *The Spirituality*, 252.
44 *1N* 6,1-8.
45 *3A* 19,8.
46 B. Dent, *My Only Friend*, 38-39.
47 T. Spidlík, *The Spirituality*, 250.
48 *1N* 7,2-5.
49 *1N* 7,2.
50 *1N* 6,1-8.
51 T. Spidlík, *The Spirituality*, 249.
52 *1N* 41-8.
53 B. Dent, *My Only Friend*, 39-41.
54 *3A* 20,3.
55 *3A* 26,2-6.
56 *Sayings* 112.
57 *1A* 6,5.
58 *3A* 36,3-5.
59 *3A* 18,1.
60 *2A* 24,1.
61 *Sayings* 24.
62 *3A* 5,1; 27,1-29,5.
63 *3A* 30,1-32,4.
64 1 Cor. 12.
65 D.B. Tillyer, *Union with God*, 85-86.
66 *3A* 33,1-5.
67 *2A* 21,4.
68 *Interior Castle* 1,2. *The Collected Works of St Teresa of Avila* (tr., K. Kavanaugh and O. Rodriguez), (Washington, D.C. ICS Publications, 1980), Vol. 2, 295.
69 *2A* 16,6.
70 *2A* 16,7.
71 *1N* 2,1-8; *3A* 9,1-2; *1N* 12,8.
72 *1N* 2,2.
73 *1N* 2,3.
74 *1N* 7,1-5.
75 *1N* 7,1.
76 B. Dent, *My Only Friend*, 43-44.
77 *1N* 5,1-3.
78 *1N* 5,2.
79 *1N* 5,3.
80 *1N* 3,1-3; *1N* 6,1-8.
81 *1N* 6,1.
82 *1N* 6,1-8; *1N* 7,1-5.
83 B. Dent, *My Only Friend*, 42.
84 *1N* 6,3.

85 *1N* 4,1-8.
86 *2N* 2,3.
87 *3A* 31,1-9.
88 *2A* 11,7.
89 D. B. Tillyer, *Union with God,* 88.
90 *3A* 30,4.
91 *2A* 29,5.
92 *3A* 28,1-9.
93 *2A* 19,7-8.
94 F. Ruiz, *God Speaks in the Night,* 313.
95 *Sayings* 54.
96 *LF* 2,25.
97 *2A* 11,10; *1N* 14,4; *1N* 10,1.
98 Barbara Dent gives a picturesque presentation of the *nada* experience in her book *My Only Friend is Darkness* with the help of an analogy, B. Dent, *My Only Friend,* 29-30.
99 *C* 16,10.
100 *Sayings* 55.
101 *Sayings* 51.
102 *Sayings* 53.
103 *LF* 1,32.
104 *1A* 4,1.
105 R. Collings, *John of the Cross* (Collegeville, Minnesota: Michael Glazier Book, 1990), 64.
106 N. Cummins, *Freedom to Rejoice,* 76.
107 *C* 1,8.
108 *Sayings* 77.
109 *Sayings* 92.
110 To get a very concise view of John's attitude towards suffering, cf. *C* 36,12.
111 *3A* 38,3.
112 *Sayings* 121.
113 *Sayings* 95.
114 *Sayings* 91.
115 *Sayings* 171.
116 *Sayings* 154.
117 *Sayings* 124.
118 *Sayings* 153.
119 *3A* 6,1-4; *1N* 10,4; *LF* 3,33-43.
120 H. Bacovcin (tr.), *The Way of the Pilgrim and The Pilgrim Continues His Way* (New York: Image Books, 1992), 114-16.
121 *Prec* 13.
122 L. of St Joseph, *The Secret of Sanctity,* 88.
123 *1N* 12,7-8.
124 L. of St Joseph, *The Secret of Sanctity,* 92.
125 *2N* 10,9; *C* 36,12.
126 *C* 1,7; *LF* 3,80; 4,15.

127 *C* 22,4-7; 26,5-8.
128 *C* 22,5.
129 *2N* 2-3; 12,1-7; 17,6.
130 *1A* 13,11.
131 *3A* 19,4-11; 44,2-3; *1A* 4,8.
132 *2A* 24,9; *2A* 29,12; *3A* 6,1-4; *3A* 28,7.
133 *1A* 5,1; *2A* 5,7; *3A* 16,1; *1N* 4,7; *C* 1,14; 26,5-10; 28,1.
134 *1N* 3,2.
135 *2A* 17,8-9; *3A* 35,7-8; *1N* 11,1-7.
136 *1A* 14,2.
137 *2A* 1,2.
138 *2N* 11,7.
139 i.e. charity, joy, peace, patience, kindness, goodness, generosity, gentleness, faithfulness, modesty, self-control, chastity. Cf. Galatians 5:22-23, Latin Vulgate version.
140 *1N* 13,11.
141 *2A* 5,7.
142 *C* 24,8.
143 *1N* 13,3.
144 *C* 15,22.
145 *2A* 5,4.
146 *1A* 11,4.
147 *2N* 18,2-5.

THREE

THE PROGRESSIVE STEPS OF *NADA*

Introduction

John regards the call to *nada* as a universal call, which is shared by all. Since God has called everything into existence from *nada*, the basic reality of everything is *nada*. Any attempt at self-discovery or self-realisation naturally leads the person to their origin, which is *nada*. Normally, however, people are reluctant to encounter or accept their nothingness. It appears that humanity has inherited from its first parents the desire to be like God (Gen 3:5). God being the owner of everything, it is natural that those who wish to be like him want to own as much as possible. Possessing material as well as spiritual goods is often considered as the best way to attain equality with God or at least show one's worth to God and others. Thus, by following the paths of the imperfect spirits people try to improve their virtuousness before God and their fellows. Even their devotion to God is often motivated by self-interest, love and devotion being the bait that people often use to 'hook' God on their line. For many believers God is like the 'sacred cow' of Hindu mythology, that is capable of fulfilling all their desires if properly caressed. Such people think that if not treated adequately, God may cause trouble and make them suffer. This kind of spirituality is guided by the pleasure-pain principle, extended beyond the boundaries of our earthly existence. John does not hold this opinion: genuine spiritual life begins only with an experience of *nada* and it reaches its perfection in the total nakedness of spirit. A person on the true spiritual path shows an openness to the truth, that is, a voluntary acceptance of their own nothingness, so that the reality – *el todo* – may shine through their life. In such a person there exists no more greed, fear, or anxiety concerning the future.

Nada is the path of the 'brave heart', demanding purification, emptying, and a total annihilation of the self. John writes, "No creature, none of its actions and abilities, can reach or encompass God's nature."[1] John here proclaims the absolute necessity of a person's entry into *nada* for experiencing *el todo*. The example of Jesus on the cross gives us a model for the perfect self-surrender and total self-negation that merits God's acceptance. There was nothing in Jesus contrary to the will of his heavenly Father, and so he could claim, "I am in the Father and the Father is in me" (Jn 14:11). John never wavers in his insistence on self-negation. The path of the perfect spirit is a walk in *nada*, towards *nada*. Progression on the path of *nada* is gradual, starting with the purification of the sensory faculties and continued by that of the spiritual faculties.

Though the call to sanctity is universal, we do not see many pilgrims on the path of *nada*, according to John the sure route to sanctity and perfect union with God. The reason for this is not that God wishes only a few to be elevated to this lofty state. As John puts it, "He would rather want all to be perfect, but he finds few vessels that will endure so lofty and sublime a work. Since he tries them in little things and finds them so weak that they immediately flee from work, unwilling to be subject to the least discomfort and mortification."[2] The vessel must be strong in order to hold a full measure of God's self-communication. God wants to give more, but weak human beings detest the strengthening process, as John explains in the following passage:

> There are many who desire to advance and persistently beseech God to bring them to this state of perfection. Yet when God wills to conduct them through the initial trials and mortifications, as is necessary, they are unwilling to suffer them and they shun them, flee from the narrow road of life (Mt 7:14) and seek the broad road of their own consolation, which is that of their own perdition (Mt 7:13); thus they do not allow God to begin to grant their petition. They are like useless containers, for although they desire to reach the state of the perfect, they do not want to be guided by the path of trials that leads to it. They hardly even begin to walk along this road by submitting to what is least, that is, to ordinary suffering.[3]

Union with God requires discipline. This discipline aims at the transformation of two areas of human life, namely, the sensory self and the spiritual self. The sensory self is disciplined through the mortification of the desires belonging to the exterior and interior sense-faculties, aided by the evangelical counsels: chastity, obedience, and poverty. The spiritual self is disciplined by a living of the theological virtues: faith, hope, and charity. John is of course using terminology traditional in the Catholic Church, at times bewildering in its detail, but his 'system' is in fact original and unique, developed largely on the basis of his own personal experience rather than depending on a previously existing system.

Traditional stages of spiritual progress

From the earliest days of Christianity, spiritual writers have divided the progress of a person towards their final destiny into three stages or ways – the purgative, the illuminative, and the unitive. The first stage is dominated by fear, the second by hope, and the third by love. While the majority of writers use this threefold division as descriptive of ordinary Christian life in its normal stages, others like Pseudo-Dionysius and John of the Cross use these same terms in a restricted sense. The beginners, according to Pseudo-

Dionysius and John, are not those who enter the way of purification seeking to be purified from those sins Catholic Tradition has called 'mortal' (meaning an act which is gravely wrong, performed with full consent and knowledge; in carrying out this act the person turns definitely away from God, and it requires a new initiative of God's mercy to call them back[4]), but those who, having already attained what is ordinarily called the way of illumination, now seek to go further. The beginners of Pseudo-Dionysius and John are those who are already on the path of the spirit; for them, progress means to be brought to the painful recognition of their hidden motives of ego-worship and the need to acquire. Previously feeling themselves to be doing well, the person is now brought by means of contemplative aridity into a habitual sense of their need for purification, and thus "considering themselves now nothing and having no satisfaction in themselves; for they see that of themselves they do nothing, nor can do anything."[5]

Characteristics of the beginners

John, in fact, says very little about conversion, presumably because he was writing for those who had already committed themselves in faith within the Discalced reform of the Carmelite Order. Nevertheless, he does provide a detailed analysis of the period after conversion because it is a critical stage that lays down the foundations for further development. Of course, Christian life essentially begins at the font; regeneration in baptism is the beginning of the road to union with God. In practice, however, not all people are on the path of *nada*, not even on the path of the spirit. John recognises that the spiritual life begins in earnest only when a Christian turns to God seriously, determined to give themselves to the service of God in total commitment, prepared to face the cost of discipleship. The significant point here is that conversion does not in fact change the relationship which exists between God and a person through Baptism: for those who are baptised, conversion is nothing but taking the fact of regeneration seriously. There are certain attitudes a person has to develop and certain conditions to fulfil in order to be recognised as a true seeker on the path of the spirit. We have already noted that even on this path of the spirit we may come across different types of seekers who can be distinguished on the basis of their differing motivations. As explained in the previous chapter, there are seekers who prefer to gather either the goods of earth or those of heaven on their Godward journey. There are a few who dare to follow the path of *nada* in their quest for God. As the introduction to the first stanza of *Canticle*, John gives a brief but full account of the prerequisites for undertaking the spiritual journey:

> The soul at the beginning of this song has grown aware of her obligations and observed that life is short (Jb 14:5), the path leading to eternal life constricted (Mt 7:14), the just one scarcely saved (1 Pt 4:18), the things of the world vain and deceitful (Eccl 1:2), that all comes to an end and fails like falling water (2 Sam 14.14), and that the time is uncertain, the accounting strict, perdition very easy, and salvation very difficult. She knows on the other hand of her immense indebtedness to God for having created her solely for himself, and that for this she owes him the service of her whole life; and because he redeemed her solely for himself she owes him every response of love. She knows, too, of the thousand other benefits by which she has been obligated to God from before the time of her birth, and that a good part of her life has vanished, that she must render an account of everything – of the beginning of her life as well as the later part – unto the last penny (Mt 5:26), when God will search Jerusalem with lighted candles (Zeph 1:12), and that it is already late – and the day far spent (Lk 24:29) – to remedy so much evil and harm. She feels on the other hand that God is angry and hidden because she desired to forget him so in the midst of creatures. Touched with dread and interior sorrow of heart over so much loss and danger, renouncing all things, leaving aside all business, and not delaying a day or an hour,

with desires and sighs pouring from her heart, wounded now
with love for God, she begins to call her Beloved.[6]

The attitude found in the person starting out on the
true spiritual path leads them to form for themselves a
specific lifestyle in which they find sweetness in anything
that pertains to God. A desire for mental prayer and a life
of devotion will blossom. Meditation will become
spontaneous and natural and so will a strong faith in the
loving mercy of God. A consciousness of their own sinfulness
and worthlessness emerges in the person as the result of an
increased self-understanding. This awareness leads to a
strong desire for change in lifestyle so as to follow the will
of God more closely. This alternative lifestyle that is being
developed is nothing but the lifestyle of our Lord Jesus
Christ – a life remarkable for its purity of heart: "How
happy are the pure in heart, they shall see God" (Mt 5:8),
as it is impurity that alienates one from God. Purity can be
reached and maintained by dissociating ourselves from all
impurities and through avoiding further contamination.
John insists that no one should expect union with the
divine lover in an 'impure bed':

> One cannot reach this union without remarkable purity, and
> this purity is unattainable without vigorous mortification and
> nakedness regarding creatures... Persons who refuse to go out at
> night in search of the beloved and to divest and mortify their
> will, but rather seek the Beloved in their own bed and comfort,
> as did the bride (Sg 3:1), will not succeed in finding him. As
> this soul declares, she found him when she departed in darkness
> and with longings of love.[7]

John's psychology

As in the case of his theology, John's psychology is rooted
in the thought of Thomas Aquinas and Scholasticism. But
unlike Scholastic theology, Scholastic psychology does not
have a clear-cut and universally accepted terminology. The

general ideas of this psychology were held in common, but each theologian developed his own psychological language, as John himself did. Since the psychological model used by John was very different from the one used in the twentieth century, we will have to forget, as far as possible, the current terminology and its presuppositions. For here we are dealing with a pre-Freudian analysis of the human psyche: many modern psychological terms, such as, 'emotion', 'mind', 'unconscious' and 'personality' find virtually no place in John's vocabulary, and to complicate matters further, some commonplace terms, such as 'imagination' and 'memory', are used in a sense quite different from that which we use in ordinary life. Given this, it is probably better to concentrate on how John understood the human person rather than attempting to translate his terms into modern psychological language.[8]

In John's psychology, the human person is divided into three parts. The major division is that between body and soul. The soul in its turn is divided into a lower, sensitive part and a higher part called the spirit. The soul governs the body.[9] The lower level or part of the soul is called the animal soul or the sensitive part; at this level the soul is directly in touch with the body through the senses. The senses are themselves of two kinds. First, there are the five 'exterior bodily senses', that is, the senses of sight, hearing, taste, smell and touch. Each of these exterior bodily senses in the animal soul corresponds to a sensory organ of the body. In addition to these the animal soul possesses two 'interior bodily senses' called imagination and fantasy. It may seem strange that John places the faculty of imagination in the animal soul, but he does so because of the Scholastic theory of knowledge, according to which imagination is an internal sense that simply combines any 'external' experiences we may have in different configurations. There is nothing rational in itself in this process. The second interior bodily sense, fantasy, is simply the ability to stabilise or hold an image from the imagination so that it can be considered at length. Thus, the sensitive part of the soul receives information through its five exterior and two interior bodily senses and prepares the material for further assessment.

This assessment occurs at the second level of operation, which John calls the higher part of the soul. This higher part is the place of the rational or spiritual faculties, which according to John are three in number: memory, understanding and will. John sees all these faculties as 'intellectual faculties' or 'spiritual faculties'. Memory is the spiritual faculty that works in close co-operation with imagination and the exterior bodily senses. One of its functions is to store up the information and images gathered by means of the five senses or obtained supernaturally.[10] The memory not only recalls past experiences, but also looks forward to the future based on the material received in the past. The understanding is the faculty that is identical with the modern psychological term 'intellect', and John often uses the latter term. All the three faculties of the spirit are rational, but the understanding is distinguished from the memory and the will by its ability to comprehend. It is the seat of logical thinking. There is an intimate collaboration between the memory and the understanding for the purpose of producing knowledge. This knowledge is then stored in the memory. The third faculty of the spirit is the will, which is the power of the person. The will governs the whole personality by gathering up and directing the powers of the soul. While the rest of the creation is subject to the law of cause and effect, human beings are able to break out of that circular process by rational thought and action. We are endowed with free will and are able to make free choices of our own volition, or at least, ideally that is so: in practice, however, the ideal is rarely the case, because original sin has played havoc with humanity and its capacity for true freedom. As a result, inordinate desires and passions dominate the will.[11] God's grace is the only way that a person can be lifted out of this human 'fallenness': through willed co-operation with grace, they are able to advance towards union with God. In this process ordinary 'natural' ways of receiving are inadequate when it comes to receiving things from God:[12] the receiver must be tuned into God's wavelength to be able to distinguish it from the cacophony coming from the world. "All that is not God"[13] becomes a hindrance to the realisation of union. The solution of the problem is to get rid of 'all that is not God', that is, all thoughts, visions, forms, images, concepts and the like, from the soul, and keep it in total darkness. John explains it as follows:

> the preparation for this union, as we said, is not an understanding by the soul, nor the taste, feeling, or imagining of God or of any other object, but purity and love, the stripping off and perfect renunciation of all such experiences for God alone. Also we clearly see how perfect transformation is impossible without perfect purity, and how the illumination of the soul and its union with God correspond to the measure of its purity. The illumination will not be perfect until the soul is entirely cleansed, clear, and perfect.[14]

To empty, purify or denude the soul of its objects is to turn its attention from the exterior appearances of objects to discover something of God at their ground or root. We can actively work for the development of such a consciousness by striving to collaborate with the grace of God in seeking the virtues of faith, hope and charity. The person does not develop these virtues out of nothing; being related to the soul's own faculties, each virtue transforms them and aligns them with God's purpose, promoting union between the person and their Creator, so that they will what God wills and reject what God rejects. John developed his psychology with the conviction that we have our part to play in the movement towards union, but he did not fail to remind us that our knowledge, however sublime it may be, falls short of revealing God:

> However elevated God's communications and the experiences of his presence are, and however sublime a person's knowledge

of him may be, these are not God essentially, nor are they
comparable to him because, indeed, he is still hidden to the
soul. Hence, regardless of all these lofty experiences, a person
should think of him as hidden.[15]

Asceticism as the application of *nada* to 'ordinary' life

For John spiritual progress corresponds to the emptying of
the self of all that is not God. The human soul, as we have
noted, is composed of sensory and spiritual parts.[16] The
emptying of the former is mainly done through traditional
asceticism (asceticism being, roughly, a 'training' that the
believer undertakes at God's invitation to combat the
destructive tendencies within them and prepare themselves
for deeper communion with God, and includes traditional
practices such as fasting from food), while the emptying of
the latter is achieved through what in John's language is
called 'non-discursive contemplation' (a kind of prayer
where the understanding is not active and communications
from God are received directly into the spiritual part of the
soul). The animal or sensual part of the soul is the abode of
passions and affections. But what does John mean when he
refers to passions and affections? Passions are movements
in the animal soul which arise under the influence of sense-
experience and cause us to react in particular ways. They
are natural and involuntary acts, spontaneous inclinations
that arise out of the animal soul and have no rationality
about them. If these passions are accepted by the spirit,
however, they are rationalised. A passion thus accepted by
the spirit is known as an affection, and in particular, an
affection of the will. We have here the same distinction
that exists between the exterior and interior bodily senses
of the animal soul and the intellectual faculties of the spirit.
Thus a passion received and accepted by the spirit is diffused
into the memory and understanding to become the basis of
the activity by the will. Thus it becomes an influence upon

the will in its decision-making, and thereby affects the ability of the will to be the 'master of its own house'. The passions and affections of the soul together constitute what we call the emotions. They are morally neutral in themselves and, therefore, their influence can be for the good or the bad. They develop, either as virtues or as vices, depending on how the will acts upon them.

John describes the passions under four headings: joy, hope, sorrow and fear.[17] The names of the first two are perplexing, shocking even, since they usually refer to two great Christian virtues. In the context of discussing the passions, however, these terms mean quite different things. Thus, joy is simply the delight in a basic sensual pleasure; hope is the expectation of repeating that pleasure again; sorrow is the involuntary misery which follows a hurt or a pleasure denied; and finally, fear is the anticipation of such hurt or deprivation. Joy and hope are positive passions; sorrow and fear are their negative counterparts. All these passions are morally neutral. What is important is what we do with them: they may develop into vices if they get out of hand, or, if the will is able to restrain them and channel their energies they become the source of all virtues.[18] John uses strong language regarding the desires enkindled in the person by the passions and affections, when these latter two are no longer controlled by the will:

> The desires weary and fatigue the soul; for they are like restless and discontented children, who are ever demanding this or that from their mother, and are never satisfied... Fire goes down when the wood is consumed, but desire, though it increases when the fuel is added to it, decreases not correspondingly when the fuel is consumed; on the contrary, instead of going down, as does the fire when its fuel is consumed, it fails from weariness, for its hunger is increased and its food diminished.[19]

The moment of danger comes, as we have seen, when malicious desires pass over into the rational soul and become affections of the will. Once this happens, habits are beginning to form, bonds are being made, and attitudes created, all of which can drag the person into imperfection and sin. To feel a natural desire rising spontaneously within the animal soul is one thing; to accept it as a desire worthy of pursuit is another. Therefore, John insists, "Voluntary desires, whether they be of... sin... or whether they be only of imperfections... must be driven away".[20] The important qualifying word here is 'voluntary', that is, of the will. Here we must notice that John does not ask us to suppress or deny what is good and natural, he only recommends that it should be brought in line with the will as it seeks the will of God. John holds that sin lies wholly in the will, just as all the virtues depend on the will for their origin and development:[21]

> They are of the opinion that any kind of withdrawal from the world, or reformation of life, suffices. Some are content with a certain degree of virtue, perseverance in prayer, and mortification, but never achieve the nakedness, poverty, selflessness, or spiritual purity (which are all the same)...[22] The road and ascent to God, then, necessarily demand a habitual effort to renounce and mortify the appetites; the sooner this mortification is achieved, the sooner the soul reaches the top. But until the appetites are eliminated, one will not arrive no matter how much virtue is practised. For one will be failing to acquire perfect virtue, which lies in keeping the soul empty, naked, and purified of every appetite.[23]

In John's vision, active purification is the human task in which the person opens themselves to God's action through poverty of spirit, while passive purification is the effect of God's action in the person. A decrease of 'I' (self) comes before an increase of 'he' (God) (cf. Jn 3:30). John proposes the method of radical detachment from all creatures so that in its affections the person may be free for God:

> Endeavour to be inclined always: not to the easiest, but to the most difficult; not to the most delightful, but to the most distasteful; not to the most gratifying, but to the less pleasant;

not to what means rest for you, but to hard work; not to the consoling, but to the unconsoling; not to the most, but to the least; not to the highest and most precious, but to the lowest and most despised; not to wanting something, but to wanting nothing. Do not go about looking for the best of temporal things, but for the worst, and, for Christ, desire to enter into complete nakedness, emptiness, and poverty in everything in the world.[24]

These maxims are meant to create in the seeker a radical spirit of asceticism. The road or ascent to God, then, necessarily demands a habitual effort to renounce and mortify (subdue and bring under control by self-denial and so on) the appetites. "It should be noted", wrote John, "that all the harm the soul receives is born of its enemies... the world, the devil, and the flesh".[25] These three enemies of the soul exercise their dominion by means of the four passions (joy, hope, fear, and sorrow). When their promises and temptations fail to bring about the desired effect, they employ threats and warnings. The world, for example, attempts to intimidate the soul

principally in three ways. First, it makes her think she must live without its favour, and lose her friends, reputation, importance and even wealth. Second, through another beast, no less ferocious, it makes her wonder how she will ever endure the permanent lack of consolation and delights of the world and all its comforts. Third, which is still worse, it makes her think that tongues will rise up against her and mock her, there will be many remarks and jeers, and she will be considered almost worthless.[26]

Ascetical practices of a harsh nature were never endorsed by John. Such practices, without the assistance of God's grace, could never be an effective means towards union with him: "You should not use any force except to detach your soul and liberate it, so as not to alter its peace and tranquillity."[27] All extremes of bodily penance are vicious and even counterproductive.[28] Similarly, John did not think that flight from the world would solve the problem of attachment:

> we are not discussing the mere lack of things; this lack will not divest the soul if it craves for all these objects. We are dealing with the denudation of the soul's appetites and gratifications... Since the things of the world cannot enter the soul, they are not in themselves an encumbrance or harm to it; it is the will and appetite dwelling within that cause the damage when set in these things.[29]

Scattered acts of desire are harmless compared to habitual appetites which lead to an automatic acting out of various desires. Appetites that are grounded in God and find satisfaction, without attachment, in all their objects, do not blind and enslave a person.

No one attains God fully, except through "an intimate nakedness, purgation, and spiritual hiding from all that is of creatures".[30] When the person is "buffeted and purged through the war of the dark night in a twofold way (in the sensory and spiritual parts with their senses, faculties, and passions)", they attain "a twofold peace and rest in the faculties and appetites of both the sensory and spiritual parts of their soul".[31] When these two parts of the person are wholly at rest and strengthened, and the faculties and appetites have been put to sleep regarding earthly and heavenly things, too, God's wisdom is united with the soul in a new bond of the possession of love.[32]

Asceticism, thus, is a process that involves different stages. It is a passage of the person from the control of the senses to the control of their own will, and finally to the control of God's will. Being controlled by God's will makes the person free to be controlled by the needs of the other. The final stage of this process is total freedom. Genuine detachment means the death of preferences of all kinds – even of those which would seem to other people the very proofs of virtue and fine taste.[33]

The effects of asceticism

As we have observed earlier, for John spiritual progress entails the painful recognition of hidden motives: a need to acquire and to have egos continually boosted, even in the things of the spirit. Through renunciation the person progresses, but the 'departure' is not from the material realm alone: *nada* has to be applied to anything and everything that is not God. Everything can be measured by one single criterion alone: does this 'object' in my life – whether material, spiritual, divine or satanic – lead to our ultimate aim, *el todo?* Renunciation causes suffering, and the cross stands for suffering and renunciation. Renunciation, therefore, joins the person with Jesus. Jesus, on the cross, underwent suffering of the utmost deprivation in his sensory as well as spiritual natures. The effect of this total negation on the intellect is darkness. A mind that refuses to use images and discursive reasoning is in the dark. 'Dark night' is thus a description of an experience as well as a metaphor, representing attitudes and ideas related to this experience. John gives other reasons also for naming this experience dark night. He says, "individuals must deprive themselves of their appetites for worldly possessions. This denial and deprivation are like a night for all one's senses."[34]

Ascetical practice also generates in the person a sense of spiritual emptiness.[35] Such a person recognises the will of God as the unique source of all meaning and so, freely relinquishing the control of their life to God, enters a region not of uncertainty, but of great mystery.[36] John perceives mystery as something that transcends human reason, that is, something that surpasses human comprehension without flatly denying it. The emptiness of the spirit which he proclaims, that is, the total docility to God's action, is not a desperate submission to an inscrutable and tyrannical divine will. It is in fact the net result of a perfect self-knowledge and the resultant readiness to accept a more reasonable way. It is the ultimate human wisdom to abandon oneself to divine providence, to let God be in charge of one's destiny.[37]

The preliminary steps

The 'stilling' of the house that John talks about in the poem 'Dark Night' is the first part of the exciting spiritual adventure.[38] The person must, indeed, strive with all their energy to be delivered from the fetters of their own sensual nature, but only with God's assistance progress is achieved. Detachment from the things of the world is the point of departure. In John's view true 'spiritual persons' are those highly favoured ones whom God has put on the path of *nada* that leads to the summit of the mount, which is the total nakedness of the spirit. In fact, they are already detached to a great extent from the temporal things of this world.[39] As noted before, John's writings concentrate on such spiritually enthusiastic 'young adults', who have already set their feet on the path of self-negation. What John offers them is "substantial and solid doctrine",[40] which will guide them along the path of *nada* towards the total nakedness of spirit. In following these guidelines they must strive hard to liberate themselves from the clutches of the inordinate passions by co-operating with God's initiative. This is the way of the faith, which offers no reason, no assurance, nor anything else to hold on to. Because this type of renunciation produces an experience of darkness and nothingness in the person, this spiritual journey takes the path into the dark night. When the world of the senses is left behind, the person begins to experience the dusk – the beginning of the night. Eventually, they enter the midnight darkness of faith. Faith, in turn, blinds the person by taking away not only the activity of the senses but also the natural knowledge of reason: but when the person experiences the presence of God in this darkness, it seems as if the dawn of the new day of eternity were already breaking into their night.[41]

Now we will turn to look at the preliminary steps of this journey: almost all religions recommend in some form the practice of chastity, obedience and poverty, called in Christianity the evangelical counsels. Their practice is a means of breaking free from the involuntary behavioural framework that restricts us, or, to put it in a more traditionally Christian way, to remove whatever might hinder the development of charity (even if what is removed is not contrary to charity). The Christian understanding is that Christ proposes these counsels in various appropriate ways to every disciple, so they can be practised overtly and fully in a group like a Religious Order or in an adapted way compatible with different lifestyles, such as the married state.[42]

Christian spirituality has traditionally spoken of three spiritual enemies: the world, the flesh and the devil, which control our natural and involuntary ways of thinking. John was convinced that by controlling the senses, one can control the mind and thus acquire purity of soul. He called the senses the "gates of the soul".[43] In our ordinary day-to-day life we allow ourselves to be guided by innumerable habits formed by the social and cultural conditions in which we live. In order to enter *nada* consciousness, which is a condition opposite to the ordinary mentality, the person has to break with the normal behavioural pattern. In his *Precautions*, the much condensed presentation of his doctrine, John sets chastity, obedience and poverty against each of those three enemies. Chastity guards against the concupiscence of the flesh, obedience, against the traps of the devil, and poverty against the temptations of the world.[44] *Canticle* presents a girl that refrains from the temptation of gathering flowers. The flowers stand for gratifications, satisfactions, and delights, which are of three kinds: temporal, sensory and spiritual, all of which are capable of occupying the heart and hindering the spiritual nakedness which is essential for union with the beloved.[45] John uses the following analogy to express the fundamental importance of active purification:

> As the tilling of soil is necessary for its fruitfulness – untilled soil produces only weeds – mortification of the appetites is necessary for one's spiritual fruitfulness. I venture to say that without this mortification all that is done for the sake of advancement in perfection and in knowledge of God and of oneself is no more profitable than seed sown on uncultivated ground. Accordingly, darkness and coarseness will always be with the soul until its appetites are extinguished. The appetites are like a cataract on the eye or specks of dust in it; until removed they obstruct vision.[46]

John did not write specifically about these evangelical counsels. This is probably because certain works, *Ascent* for example, were addressed not to everybody, "but only some of the persons of our holy order of the primitive observance of Mount Carmel, both friars and nuns".[47] The individuals in question were either living the consecrated life and had explicitly taken these counsels upon themselves or were closely associated with such people (Doña Ana, for example, to whom *Living Flame* was addressed) and so in each case a familiarity with them could be presumed upon.

Of the three counsels, chastity comes before obedience and poverty because it is the parting point with the 'ways of the world'. In fact, the practising of chastity *in celibacy for the sake of the Kingdom* is the determining commitment of the state of consecrated life, while those in other states of life are called to live it in other forms suitable for their way of life. Chastity is the evangelical counsel that most obviously shows the power of grace, which raises love beyond the human being's natural inclinations. Chastity is purity,[48] and becomes ever more profound as the person advances in *nada*. It begins, however, with a simple bodily negation of improper appetites. Obedience, the second step, is the practice of and the means to the ultimate goal of spiritual poverty or the nakedness of spirit. Obedience is practised through self-negation in everyday life. The place of poverty in these preliminary steps is last, since poverty is the goal of the previous two virtues. As Evelyn Underhill puts it:

Those three virtues which the instinct of the Catholic Church fixed upon as the necessities of the cloistered life – the great Evangelical counsel of voluntary Poverty with its departments, Chastity, the poverty of the senses, and Obedience, the poverty of the will – are also, when raised to their highest term and transmitted by the Fire of Love, the essential virtue of the mystical quest... Their common characteristic is this: they tend to make the subject regard itself, not as an isolated and interesting individual, possessing desires and rights, but as a scrap of the Cosmos, an ordinary bit of the Universal Life, only important as a part of All, an expression of the Will Divine.[49]

Chastity is undividedness. In its final state, chastity is the crystal purity of the person's heart, cleansed from the personal desires and virgin to all but God.[50] Obedience is the abnegation of selfhood through the mortification of the will which results in a complete self-abandonment, a 'holy indifference' to the accidents of life. Poverty is an utter self-stripping, the casting off of material as well as spiritual wealth, a complete detachment from all finite things. These three aspects of perfection are really one: linked together as irrevocably as the three aspects of the self.

Chastity

Though as we have just seen, John probably did not feel the need to introduce his readers to the counsel of chastity, this does not mean that he avoided the subject, it being a fundamental theme in his writings. John presents chastity as an impenetrable fortress against the enchantments of the flesh, and equates it with purity, which is an essential condition for union with God. He distinguishes two different expressions of purity: bodily and spiritual.[51] Chastity is the undivided attention of the person to their beloved by avoiding distracting pleasures. Chastity, by refusing to be distracted by pleasure, is a self-surrender, "keeping nothing back".[52] Chastity does not preclude the

love between individuals of the opposite sex, but only
those relationships which alienate from the love of God.
Any relationship that originates from self-centeredness and
leads to the exclusion of others is against chastity, which
blossoms in true friendship. Chastity shows the disciple
how to follow and imitate Jesus, who has chosen us as his
friends, who has given himself totally to us and allows us to
participate in his Sonship.[53] Chastity enables a person to
overcome any element of disordered passion that may
creep into love relationships: it is they who own their
sexuality, and not the other way round. Chastity means the
integration of sexuality within the person. It includes an
apprenticeship in self-mastery.[54] Those who profess chastity
within a permanent way of life recognised by the Church
find that this counsel liberates them in a unique way,
keeping them from the immersion in the innumerable
preoccupations of family and 'secular' life that threatens to
divide their hearts, and allowing them to dedicate themselves
to the two concerns of charity: God and all that God
loves.[55] Christ is the model of chastity, and every baptised
person is called to follow him in the chaste life, each
according to their particular state of life.[56] By pronouncing
nada to the inappropriate desires and fears of body and
mind, chastity equips the person for self-control. Chastity
is the result of finding the "hidden treasure" (Mt 13:44),
for the possession of which all else is considered *nada*.
Chastity is a prerequisite for achieving Christian perfection.

John did not insist on virginity (virginity, that is,
consecrated to God) as an essential constituent of the path
of *nada*, though he was very much convinced of its
advantages.[57] John speaks of the futility of the virginity
preserved by the five foolish virgins.[58] Freedom to
concentrate all energies on seeking union with God is a
major value that derives from consecrated virginity.[59]
Virginity does not imply contempt of the body, and is not
a form of escapism but a means of total availability to God
and to people. The invitation of the Kingdom of God casts

such a spell on certain persons that they leave everything joyfully without counting the cost (Lk 14:26; 18:29). They do not cling to goods and possessions any more (Mk 10:21), nor can they be anxious about seeking their own livelihood (Mk 8:34). Sexual abstinence is often rated as the chief element of virginity, but this attitude proceeds from the mistaken notion that sexual abstinence in itself is pre-eminent over sexual activity. Genital sexual abstinence is a consequence of virginity and not its constituent factor. In fact, virginity is not a natural endowment but a virtue to be acquired. True virginity is an answer to God's call to *nada*. It is the gift of self to God. Always immersed in God, the virgin becomes more and more sensitive to goodness and beauty and responds ever more easily and fully to others. Slowly but effectively, such a person acquires more of the mind and heart of God and comes to see and love everything as God himself does.[60] Because of this dedication to chastity, the soul and body of the virgin are completely ordered to God and this hastens and heightens the progress towards *nada*.

Obedience

For John, obedience is the best means to practise true humility, which is the greatest weapon against the devil,[61] labelled by John as the enemy of humility.[62] True humility is the person's refusal to make themselves the centre of their world. The heart of obedience is an ardent desire to do the will of God and to make God's will the primary concern in life.[63] Obedience, in the Gospel sense, is essentially obedience to the Father as his will is manifested to us. To be disobedient is to refuse our 'transcendent' destiny, to decide for ourselves what we feel is best for us, to arrange our lives according to our own whims and fancies.[64] Obviously, when we think of the counsel of obedience we tend to associate it with those who profess it within a permanent Church-recognised state of life. Perhaps in such examples obedience is more sharply focused, but that is hardly to say that other lifestyles do not provide the chance to practise the counsel through being obedient to the demands that each state of life brings – the needs of a spouse and child, for example. With a little reflection, what John says on this topic has much to say to all kinds of people.

The first practice John recommends to fellow religious to combat the devil is that of complete and unhesitating obedience:

> Let, then, the first precaution be that, without the command of obedience, you never take upon yourself any work – apart from the obligations of your state – however good and full of charity it may seem, whether for yourself or for anyone else inside or outside the house.[65]

Obedience, in other words, is learning to tune in and listen to God's word[66] by means of self-examination and the assistance of fellow human beings (to a greater or lesser extent, depending on the relationship) to whom we hand over our prerogative of self-determination. Disobedience is the absence of faith in God and the assertion of the ego; obedience cuts right across the ego through an act of self-detachment. It is an act of self-denial and self-giving. It involves the essence of the Christian life. We do not find any occasion when Jesus set aside his perfect obedience to the Father. Obedience is a sign of total trust and confidence in the ultimate workability of God's project and an enthusiastic adherence to it. The profession of the evangelical counsel of obedience is one of the greatest aids to simplicity in religious life. John insists that perfection without obedience is impossible.[67] More than sacrifice, obedience pleases God (1 Sam 15:22). John even considered bodily penance without obedience as "no more than a penance of beasts" because "by such behaviour these persons are doing their own will".[68]

For those who have vowed to practise the counsel of obedience, it is not sufficient merely to keep this vow; it is also necessary to acquire the virtue of obedience. The vow is the means, the virtue is the end.[69] The virtue of obedience involves a total submission of the will to the design of God in faith and hope. No exterior obedience is worthwhile if it is not a reflection of an interior submission to the will of God. Humanity's fall was due to disobedience; one man's obedience to God's will saved humanity from its decadence (Rom 5:19). Kinship to Jesus is reserved for those who obey the will of the heavenly Father (Mt 12:48-50). Mary was dear to Jesus, not only because she gave birth to him, but also because she was the one who fulfilled his ideal – total submission to the will of his Father – all through her life.

The model of obedience given by John is Jesus, who took the form of a servant and "obeyed unto death"(Phil 2:8). Obedience to the Father was the food of Jesus (Jn 4:34). All through his life he was obedient to God directly (Heb 10:7; Phil 2:8) as well as indirectly, that is, through intermediaries like parents, events, institutions, inspired writings and human authorities (Lk 2:51; Mt 17:27). He came not to do his own will but the will of the one who sent him (Jn 6:38), and made his death a true sacrifice of love and obedience (Heb 10:5-10). John, in a letter to Padre Juan de Santa Ana, exhibits this very same spirit of extreme humility and self-abnegation. He wrote, "I am very ready to amend all I may have done wrong and obey in whatever penance they may give me."[70] What we accept in obedience is the programme and design of God for his creatures. For a religious, the acceptance of the wish of the superior in faith is ultimately our confidence in God's providence and not in the infallibility of the superior.

Even if your negligence amounts to no more than not being governed by obedience in all things, you culpably err, since God wants obedience more than sacrifice (1 Sam 15:22). The actions of religious are not their own, but belong to obedience, and if you withdraw from obedience, you will have to count them as lost.[71]

Obedience, when it becomes blind is inhuman and dangerous. Jesus was not obedient to every authority. He vehemently opposed those authorities who acted contrary to the ultimate authority of his Father. Christian obedience does not demand blind submission to any orders coming from any authority. By escaping from the prison cell, John demonstrated to the world that anything contrary to the law of charity does not bind. In a way, all Christian virtues are applications of the love of God in different contexts: Christian obedience is therefore a loving way of doing what pleases God. There is no predetermined pattern that governs our actions, but in every moment our actions should be guided by the law of charity. Blindness and ignorance are not corollaries of the virtue of obedience; obedience always has its eyes wide open and mind alert. Whenever and wherever love is at stake, obedience has to be reconsidered. It is the will of God that we must make the full use of our faculties and talents (Lk 19:11-27) and constantly strive to transform the world into his kingdom. If we as Christians have not been revolutionary enough, it is not because of our obedience, but because we have been insufficiently obedient to the word of God.

Poverty

John's writings do not deal with material or exterior poverty, even though from his childhood he was exposed to the pangs of it.[72] As a founding member of the Carmelite reform he opted for a strict observance of poverty[73] and had enough opportunities to experience it, but his emphasis was always on the interior poverty or the poverty of spirit.[74] For him, being totally poor means not only freeing ourselves from things but from our own selves as well.[75] By this,

John means that when the spiritual person is brought to a state of interior poverty, union with God will result.

Voluntary religious poverty is often criticised by the world because it challenges its values. In his *Precautions* John represents poverty as the strongest weapon against the attractions of the world.[76] In fact, all Christians are called to poverty (Mk 10:21). Poverty is not just the absence of necessary goods, but it is the absence of attachment to them. Everything that God created is good and has the potential to guide us to God, but anything that is used in isolation from its divine source becomes a cause of attachment and idolatry.[77] True poverty consists in giving up those things which encumber the spirit, divide its interests, and delay or halt its progress to God – whether these things be riches, habits, religious observances, friends, interests, distastes or desires – and not in mere outward destitution for its own sake. It is the attitude, not the act, that matters. Voluntary renunciation of goods of all kinds would be unnecessary were it not for our inveterate tendency to attribute false value to things the moment they become our own.[78] Voluntary acceptance of poverty is a sharing of the *kenosis* of Christ. Poverty prepares the person's spirit for that union with God to which it aspires. Poverty strips off the costumes which people often mistake for their true selves, transforms their values and shows them things as they are.[79] Those who practise poverty do not detach themselves from all the material things, but only stop being addicted and carried away by covetousness, lust, gluttony, envy, anger, sloth, pride, and the like.[80]

Advantages of material poverty

According to John, Jesus accomplished the most marvellous work of his whole life at the moment when he was the poorest, the weakest, and the most "annihilated in all things".[81] Whilst John opposed a possessive attitude, he

was never against the possession of things *per se*, either
material or spiritual. He was very practical when he spoke
of the unavoidable nature of many of our material needs.[82]
He did not advocate an irresponsible material renunciation
or expected people to renounce things that are necessary
for daily life. In fact, one of his directees was a well-to-do
laywoman (the recipient of *Living Flame*). He finds no
value in the material absence while the craving for it burns
in the heart. He was fully convinced of the claim of King
David that he was poor from his youth (Ps 88:15), since he
had not fixed his heart on riches, while being manifestly
rich. According to John, it is the state of mind that makes
one rich or poor:

> we are not discussing the mere lack of things; this lack will not
> divest the soul if it craves for all these objects. We are dealing
> with the denudation of the soul's appetites and gratifications.
> This is what leaves it free and empty of all things, even though
> it possesses them. Since the things of the world cannot enter
> the soul, they are not in themselves an encumbrance or harm to
> it; rather, it is the will and appetite dwelling within that cause
> the damage when set on these things.[83]

Human beings need possessions for survival, but not
content with simple needs they also 'need' possessions to
accumulate yet more possessions in a never-ending spiral.[84]
Wealth gives a sense of security and independence, but this
security often turns into an all-consuming preoccupation
(Lk 12:34). Riches also encourage a person to distance
themselves from others because the other becomes a threat
to their possessions, and has to be kept under constant
surveillance. God features in such a person's life only insofar
as he can guarantee prosperity and protect against threats
to this prosperity. Poverty, when practised as a virtue, has
two facets which cut across two human instincts widely
regarded as acceptable and normal even: the right ot possess
and the right to dispose of our possessions as we see fit.
The first facet of the virtue of poverty calls us to the

affective renunciation (poverty in spirit) of possession, and the second to its effective renunciation (poverty in fact). Poverty is in fact a mystical approach to detachment because it demands that anyone attempting to practise it go beyond worldly wisdom, a reliance on human resources and even the 'responsibility' of human effort by relying ultimately on, simply, the wisdom, resources and providence of God. The hope of poverty rests, finally, on the confident abandonment to the Father's providence. John, for his part, was quite convinced of the advantages of material poverty.[85]

Advantages of the poverty of spirit

The absence of material riches, however, does not always bring freedom of heart. On the contrary, it often generates a feeling of helplessness, a preoccupation with and a craving for possessions. In practice, material poverty often leads one more to bondage than to freedom. This does not mean that the acquisition of riches is the alternative, because their possession can lead a person to bondage, so that they fall into possessiveness, pride, greed and jealousy. The cultivation of the poverty of spirit is the way to escape from this vicious circle. Poverty of spirit excludes the possession by, but not of, property – making the person mistress or master of their possessions, rather than slave. The person is not free so long as the desire for things remains, while the absence of desire for things produces emptiness and freedom of soul even when there is an abundance of possessions.[86] The path that leads to poverty of spirit is an ascent to greater strength rather than a descent to utter helplessness. Poverty is a mental rather than a material state; it is an attitude. The detachment of the will from all desires of possession is the inner reality of poverty. It is with this aim in mind that John instructs spiritual directors:

Directors should strive to disencumber the soul and bring it
into solitude and idleness so that it may not be tied to any
particular knowledge, earthly or heavenly, or to any covetousness
for some satisfaction or pleasure, or to any other apprehension;
and in such a way that it may be empty through the pure
negation of every creature, and placed in spiritual poverty. This
is what the soul must do of itself, as the son of God counsels:
Whoever does not renounce the possessions cannot be my disciple
(Lk 14:33). This counsel refers not only to the renunciation
according to the will of all corporeal and temporal things, but
also to the dispossession of spiritual things, which includes
spiritual poverty, to which the Son of God ascribes beatitude
(Mt 5:3). When the soul frees itself of all things and attains to
emptiness and dispossession concerning them, which is
equivalent to what it can do of itself, it is impossible that God
fails to do his part by communicating himself to it, at least
silently and secretly.[87]

Poverty of spirit, a state in which one is "having nothing,
and yet possessing everything" (2 Cor 6:10), generates its
own transfigured joy. The ability to let go of things is the
only way of appreciating the authentic goodness of created
things. John assures us, "This person then rejoices in all
things – by not having a possessive joy in them – as if he
had them all... Having none of them in his heart, he
possesses them all, as St Paul says, in great freedom".[88] Seen
in this light, it becomes evident that John's so-called
'negative attitude' towards creation is true only when the
creation stands in the way of the Creator or, in other
words, when a person's selfishness stands in the way of
their total transformation into Christ. John sees that the
enjoyment of created gifts follows on from the removal of
possessiveness and selfishness by complete poverty of spirit.
In fact, the satisfaction of the heart is not found in the
possession of things, but in being stripped of all of them
and in the poverty of spirit. Perfection consists in the
poverty of spirit.[89]

Poverty as an experience of *nada*

John asserts that the state of spiritual childishness can be left behind only when God leads the person into the experience of *nada*. A 'spiritual cleansing' takes place as a person undergoes the *nada* experience. The person took great pains to acquire all their virtues and attracted great admiration with them: these now prove to be empty. The person's original self-perception is turned upside down, causing great dissatisfaction, amazement, and disbelief. John with a great psychological and spiritual insight describes the person's situation as follows:

> The first purgation or night is bitter and terrible to the senses. But nothing can be compared to the second, for it is horrible and frightful to the spirit... God now leaves them in such darkness that they do not know which way to turn in their discursive imaginings. They cannot advance a step in meditation, as they used to, now that the interior sense faculties are engulfed in this night. He leaves them in such dryness that they not only fail to receive satisfaction and pleasure from their spiritual exercises and works, as they formerly did, but also find these exercises distasteful and bitter. As I said, when God sees that they have grown a little, he weans them from the sweet breast so that they might be strengthened, lays aside their swaddling bands, and puts them down from his arms that they may grow accustomed to walk by themselves. This change is a surprise to them because everything seems to be functioning in reverse.[90]

The net result of such purgation is the eradication of the seven capital sins and the emergence of a sense of self-awareness. We develop a strong sense of dependence on God as we come face to face with the worthlessness and inadequacy of our personal efforts. We emerge into the world of truth (*nada*) with a readiness to abandon the 'ego' that we developed as a result of our many achievements and possessions. A correct awareness of our capacities and a realisation of the real worth of our achievements and possessions are possible only when we are cast into the furnace of *nada*. The experience of nothingness enlightens us regarding our own poverty and total dependence on God. It is a liberating experience, a freedom from the dominion of the ego. Those who encounter their own poverty through the experience of *nada,* become extremely humble:

> Now that the soul is clothed in these other garments of labour, dryness, and desolation, and its former lights have been darkened, it possesses more authentic light in this most excellent and necessary virtue of self-knowledge. It considers itself to be nothing and finds no satisfaction in self because it is aware that of itself it neither does nor can do anything.[91]

This period of dark contemplation, being a period of losing all coveted possessions, material or otherwise, is a period of great anguish. John compares this deeply experienced state of 'void' or 'suspension' to a person hanging in mid-air, unable to breathe, and with no support in sight,[92] but this extreme humiliation of the ego-self is the gateway to the realm of God where the person discovers their weakness to be a strength (cf. 2 Cor 12:10). John teaches: "He is humble who hides in his own nothingness and knows how to abandon himself to God".[93] According to John, terms like pure faith, night, poverty of the spirit, and the like all boil down to the same thing.[94] He continues:

> Poor, abandoned, and unsupported by any of the apprehensions of my soul (in the darkness of my intellect, the distress of my will, and the affliction and anguish of my memory), left to darkness in pure faith, which is a dark night for these natural faculties, and with my will touched only by sorrows, afflictions, and longings of love of God, I went out from myself.[95]

Using the example of Jesus on the cross, John equates poverty with *nada*. At the very moment in which Jesus uttered "Your will be done" (Mt 26:39), his will became inseparably united with the will of his Father. "There can be no void in nature"[96], and John suggests that absolute poverty will be refilled by God through the total gift of self.[97] Moreover, God can reveal himself as he is only to those who live in complete poverty of spirit.[98] Thus *nada* is the only 'place' where *el todo* could reveal itself unambiguously, in all its fullness. God is God only when he is not understood. God is revealed to the creatures only when they remain *nada*.[99] Those who think they are worshipping God, have often mistakenly created in their minds an image (or idol) of God that has more to do with their own desires than anything else. A person who undergoes the shattering experience of *nada* becomes aware that they had previously been practising idolatry. In the third book of *Ascent* John describes various subtle ways in which this creation of idols takes place.[100] Before having experienced *nada* it is natural for the person to reduce God to an image, a word, a thought, or a feeling they previously had of him. The 'ray of darkness' that comes to them during the dark night exposes all these attempts to capture God as nothing compared to God himself, who can be contained in "no form, figure, image or idea (whether heavenly or earthly, natural or supernatural) that can be grasped by the intellect, memory and will".[101]

The advanced steps

In his *Precautions*, John explains how chastity overcomes the concupiscence of the flesh; obedience, the snares of the devil; and poverty, the attractions of the world.[102] Thus the senses learn to accept their own limitations and inadequacies through the living of chastity, obedience and poverty, and stop resisting reality and the truth. In the preliminary stage that we have been looking at, the approach was rather 'coarse' in nature. Now begins the taming of the more spiritual faculties such as intellect, memory, and will. As we pass on to the advanced stage, we re-encounter the same old enemies – the world, the flesh, and the devil, whose tactics and weapons have become more dangerous and subtle in nature. To counter this threat, our defence plan must also be revised and improved: faith is summoned to unmask the illusions of the devil; hope is set against the attractions of the world; and charity is assigned the role of resisting the self and its egocentrism. The three interdependent theological virtues, in fact, work with the three interdependent spiritual faculties (intellect, memory and will), and guide them towards the realisation of our potential for spiritual freedom.[103] In their purity and 'objectlessness', these three virtues become a single attitude of spiritual nakedness and radical openness towards the activity of God. Thus, through poverty of spirit the theological virtues generate within a person the necessary freedom to follow the prompting of God's Spirit. John points out that these three virtues, when they are guiding a person towards *nada*, function predominantly in a negative way:

> These virtues as we said, void the faculties: Faith causes darkness and a void of understanding in the intellect, hope begets an emptiness of possessions in the memory, and charity produces the nakedness and emptiness of affection and joy in all that is not God.[104]... Faith darkens and empties the intellect of all its natural understanding and thereby prepares it for union with the divine wisdom. Hope empties and withdraws the memory from all creature possessions... and prepares the memory perfectly for union with him. Charity also empties and annihilates the affections and appetites of the will of whatever is not God, and centres them on him alone. Thus charity prepares the will and unites it with God through love. Because these virtues have the function of withdrawing the soul from all that is less than God, they consequently have the mission of joining it with God. Without walking sincerely in the grab of these three virtues, it is impossible to reach perfect union with God through love.[105]

To put it more simply, we can say that the intellect, due to its inability to comprehend God, accepts its nothingness and counts on the infinite intelligence of God with faith, in which there is no scrutinising of things but only venerating wonder.[106] Memory, as it fails to contain God within itself in some kind of natural or supernatural form, figure, image or idea, accepts its nothingness and waits in hope for a revelation from God himself.[107] Human love, which has a strong possessive tendency, accepts its nothingness after failing to entrap God, and waits at the doorstep of God, waiting for his love.[108] We may therefore conclude that all three theological virtues are positive attitudes developed as a result of the futile human attempt to possess God; they are the outcome of the *nada* experience and can be developed further only through a deeper encounter with *nada*. That is to say, as the person plunges into *nada* more and more, these three theological virtues will develop simultaneously. Not that this deepening in *nada* is a pleasant experience to the person concerned:

> Sometimes this experience is so vivid that it seems to the soul that it sees hell and perdition open before it. These are the ones who go down into hell alive (Ps 55:15), since their purgation on earth is similar to what takes place there.[109]

According to John, the three theological virtues are the means to experience nothingness and self-transcendence. But the role of these three virtues in the spiritual advancement of a person is not exhausted in the silencing of the intellect, memory and the will. They have a further important role, namely that of leading the person through *nada*. Between the person and God there exists an infinite distance. To arrive at a union between the two, a means by which this distance can be overcome must be found. Only the theological virtues present to us God, insofar as anything can, in a way that contains no error. For this reason they are the proper and suitable means to union with God. Together they purify and prepare the faculties to operate on a spiritual level through a drastic reversal of their natural operations.[110] By discontinuing the human ways of acting

through the intellect, the memory and the will, the person
starts to think only of God, remember only God and desire
only God.[111] This method of approaching God is the most
direct and the least open to the wiles of the world, the self
and the devil. It is, however, dark: no support except the
cross, no light except the dark ray of faith, and nothing to
lean upon, except hope and trust in God's love. For this
reason the whole process is a terrible experience until faith
becomes an unshakeable confidence, hope becomes a
conviction, and love becomes irresistible:

> faith is infused and rooted more deeply in the soul by means of
> that emptiness, darkness, and nakedness regarding all things, or
> by spiritual poverty (which are all the same), so too the charity
> of God is simultaneously infused and deeply rooted in the soul.
> The more individuals desire darkness and annihilation of
> themselves regarding all visions, exteriorly or interiorly receivable,
> the greater will be the infusion of faith and consequently of love
> and hope, since these three theological virtues increase
> together.[112]

Faith

Basing himself on the philosophical principle which holds
that the means must be proportionate to the end,[113] John
presents faith as an advanced step towards God. Translated
into simpler terms, we would say that in order to reach God,
the seeker should adopt a means that is capable of leading to
this end, that is, to God. Any knowledge acquired by the
intellect, any image kept in the memory, any decision taken
by the will is ultimately too 'unlike' God to lead us to him,
and can only obstruct our path. The only way left, therefore,
is to neglect the information and the data collected by these
faculties through their natural way of operating and enter
the state of unknowing and forgetfulness by surrendering
the will. This prepares the ground for contemplation. By
God's grace, if a person enters the state of *nada*, the "divine
darkness"[114] begins to feed them with a higher knowledge

through the "ray of darkness".[115] The 'ray of darkness' is so-called because it leaves no special knowledge in the intellect and no decipherable image in the memory, though it leaves an increased love and longing for God within the will. Such contemplation is a gift from God. All we can do is dispose ourselves to receive it. Using the example of the inability of a person born blind to understand the notion of colour, John sought to convince his readers of the limitations of the human intellect and the inability of human language to convey, to those who have no experience of it, a truth that has been understood through experience; and explanation is no substitute for experience.[116]

By designating faith as the "only proximate and proportionate means to the union with God", John explains that, "the likeness between faith and God is so close that no other difference exists than that between believing in God and seeing him... The greater one's faith, the closer is one's union with God."[117] To have faith is to be sure of the things we hope for, to be certain of the things that we cannot see (Heb 11:1). There are things that we believe, though they do not yield to the perception of our senses. We take them as truth because we believe in the trustworthiness of the source from which we received the information concerning them. Our source of information regarding God is the Word of God, which in Church tradition is principally to be found in Scripture.[118] Jesus, the 'Word incarnate', who is witnessed to in Scripture, proved his trustworthiness through his life, death and resurrection. Thus, Jesus is the primary source of our faith. His trustworthiness and love for us cannot be scrutinised by reason, because they cannot be measured by any direct proof. Where there is trust, there is confidence and joy that overshadow any risks that may be involved in the trusting; but where there is distrust, only fear and uncertainty prevail. Without taking the risk of trusting Jesus and following in his footsteps, nobody is able to reach the place to which he wishes to lead us.

Faith: the white tunic

John compares the three theological virtues to three
garments that protect the person from the onslaught of
their enemies.[119] These garments shield the person, and
under their cover the person's soul is invisible and
inaccessible to the destructive powers. Our three great
enemies, the world, the flesh, and the devil, want to keep
us permanently under their custody and keep watch to
prevent us from fleeing their slavery. That is why the bride
in 'Dark Night' chooses to leave the house at night while
her keepers were asleep. She prefers to use the secret ladder
for her exodus and decides to be guided by no other light
than that is burning in her heart. She clothes herself with
faith, hope and charity, the garments which are resistant
enough to protect her from the onslaught of her adversaries,
and beautiful enough to make her appealing in the eyes of
her beloved:

> Her advance in this disguise makes her more secure against her
> adversaries: the devil, the world, and the flesh. The livery she
> thus wears is of three principal colours: white, green, and red.
> These three colours stand for the three theological virtues:
> faith, hope, and charity, by which she not only gains the favour
> and good will of her Beloved but also advances very safely,
> fortified against her three enemies.[120]

John compares faith to a pure white inner tunic that
"blinds the sight of every intellect".[121] When the person is
clothed in faith the devil is ultimately powerless over them.
The person who walks in the darkness of faith, experiences
the absence of the comfort of intellectual 'light' – light that
now comes neither from above because the heaven seems
closed and God hidden, nor from below because they
derive no satisfaction from their spiritual teachers. This
experience has the advantage that it saves the person from
seeking refuge in the illusions produced by the world, the
flesh, and the devil.[122] Though John often used to compare

faith with a dark night, this darkness is, in fact, apparent only from the point of view of the human intellect. For the believer, there is no darkness, they dwell in the full light of God's revelation. Those clothed in the brilliant white tunic of faith are not easily taken in by the illusions created by their adversaries. In the same way, the brilliant white tunic of faith worn by them blinds their adversaries, and makes them unapproachable to those who would lead them astray.

Faith: the secret ladder

For John faith is also a 'secret ladder', since it guides a person beyond the boundaries of their rational nature.[123] As Pope John Paul II has said, "Faith causes the intellect to adhere not only to the revealed truths in their conceptual form, but also to the divine essence itself".[124] He continues, "Faith truly causes the intellect to transcend to the level of divinity in God, and then causes it to participate objectively in the divine essence."[125] Faith, therefore, carries the human intellect up to the level of God. Though it carries the intellect to God, it keeps the intellect in darkness. This is the reason why John compared faith to a secret ladder. Faith neither provides convincing proof to the thinking mind, nor does it produce any convincing experience to the aspiring senses. Faith is operational only in total darkness:

> The secret ladder represents faith, because all the rungs or articles of faith are secret to, and hidden from, both the senses and the intellect. Accordingly the soul lived in darkness, without any light from the senses and intellect, and went out beyond every natural and rational boundary to climb the divine ladder of faith that leads up to, and penetrates, the deep things of God (1Cor 2:10).[126]

John was very much against the habit of continually seeking apparitions and revelations, since it is against faith.

According to him, supernatural revelations had a place at the time of 'the Old Law', a time in which faith was not yet perfectly grounded, nor the Gospel law established. John clarifies his position as follows:

> But in this era of grace, now that the faith is established through Christ and the Gospel law made manifest, there is no reason for enquiring about him in this way, expecting him to answer as before. In giving us his Son, his only Word (for he possesses no other), he spoke everything to us at once in this sole Word – and he has no more to say... Those who now desire to question God or receive some vision or revelation are guilty not only of foolish behaviour but also of offending him by not fixing their eyes entirely on Christ and living with the desire for some other novelty.[127]

A little later in the same work John goes even further: "One should not believe anything coming in a supernatural way, but believe only the teachings of Christ who is human, as I say, and of his ministers who are human."[128] By ignoring the supernatural knowledge in this way, one ascends the secret ladder of faith. The degree of purity in the intellect is the same as the degree of habitual perfection of faith. The more a person is free of distinct images regarding the things of God, or in other words, the darker the spiritual landscape before them is, the more intensely and profoundly they participate objectively in God's nature.

Faith and supernatural knowledge

Normally, the intellect depends on the senses for the acquisition of information. But once the intellect submits itself by means of faith to the revelation offered through Jesus,[129] it enters the darkness of unknowing where it is given supernatural information that is incomprehensible to the normal intellect. Faith is therefore a prerequisite for gaining supernatural knowledge. In one of his lesser-known poems, called 'Stanzas Concerning an Ecstasy Experienced in High Contemplation', John explains this state of the intellect in detail, "I entered into unknowing, and there I remained unknowing, transcending all knowledge."[130] In the following eight stanzas of this poem, the phrase "transcending all knowledge" is used as a refrain to emphasise the fact that the route along which he was being led was not the route of knowledge, that is, not philosophy or theology. As John puts it, "In the night of the senses there is yet some light, because the intellect and reason remain and suffer no blindness. But this spiritual night, which is faith, removes everything, both in the intellect and in the senses."[131] In order to prepare the understanding for this union with God, the intellect must be empty of all that belongs to the senses, and be detached and freed from all that can be clearly perceived through its operations:[132]

> But all that is required for complete pacification of the spiritual house is the negation through pure faith of all the spiritual faculties and gratifications and appetites. This achieved, the soul will be joined with the Beloved in a union of simplicity and purity and love and likeness.[133]

In the spiritual night, the person possesses a knowledge of the beloved that is greater than their sorrow and enlightens their memory with hope. John calls this knowledge, faith. For him this faith is from God and *is* God, as he makes himself known in the night. The intellect, when carried up to God by means of faith, is deprived of its objects and is placed in *nada* without any ideas to hold on to. So it enters the darkness of faith, where it becomes united with God.[134] The *kenotic* attitude of pure and dark faith accompanies and reinforces the practice of imageless contemplation. The two together are able to overcome the separation of the person from God, to the awakening of faith and the practice of self-emptying:

> Like the blind, they must lean on dark faith, accept it for their
> guide and light, and rest on nothing of what they understand,
> taste, feel or imagine. All these perceptions are darkness that
> will lead them astray. Faith lies beyond all this understanding,
> taste, feeling and imagining. If they do not blind themselves in
> these things and abide in total darkness, they will not reach
> what is greater; the teaching of faith.[135]

For many people, 'faith' is nothing but an attitude by
which we accept certain propositions and concepts without
doubting their truth or questioning their validity. Faith in
John's view, however, is not merely an unquestioning,
blind submission of the intellect, but the existential attitude
of the person who transcends the limits of their intellect,
surrenders to the infinite intelligence of God and advances
along the path of *nada*. In the terminology of John, faith is
synonymous with darkness and the utter nakedness of the
soul that has detached itself from everything and which, in
the abyss of its emptiness, faces the abyss of God. Faith in
its origin, growth and perfection is a principle of
transcendence, wholly from God and wholly orientated
towards him.[136]

Hope

Hope often degenerates into a form of spiritual materialism,
a wishful clinging to the prospect of a better future. For
John, hope is openness – total availability to God. In other
words, to hope is to remain in the state of *nada*, awaiting
the realisation of God's will. Hope unites the memory with
God and empties it of all possessions.[137] Pure hope is
kenotic. To live in pure hope the person must turn to God
in loving affection, away from all the things that arise in
their mind, and remain in emptiness regarding all the
things they could remember. The more the memory gives
up possession of things, the more hope it has and, the more
hope it has, the greater will be its union with God.[138] At the

climax of hope even the intense longing for God disappears, there remains only a profound readiness to accept the will of God – whatever it may be.[139] This total acceptance of God's design leaves the person with a profound joy and peace. When the 'unknowing faith' and the 'present-centred hope' are combined with the 'totally available will' of a person, there emerges a 'readiness' which has the capacity to accommodate within it *el todo* in all its fullness. In fact, this readiness is the *nada* that waits upon *el todo*. As the *nada* experience deepens, hope too intensifies. The attainment or presence of anything that satisfies hope will make it impure and make it unworthy of hoping for the reception of *el todo*. That is the reason why pure hope alone has the power to enter the realms of *el todo*. Hope keeps us buoyant and gives us the energy to change things. The theological virtue of hope grows in the memory as the latter is emptied increasingly by the application of *nada* to the knowledge and experiences collected through the exterior and interior bodily senses. This, in turn, produces an increasing detachment from all forms of knowledge stored in the memory. This is natural and essential because God has no form or image that can be comprehended by the memory and, therefore, if the memory is to be united with God, it must become more and more detached from every particular knowledge. As we have noted, the memory is both the seat of our ability to classify and store up our sense-perceptions and knowledge gained by the understanding, and the seat of our power to anticipate the future. The memory is seen by John as the faculty upon which the grace of God moves to develop within us the virtue of hope. In hope, the memory rises above all clear knowledge and the possessions of our understanding, to the supreme hope of God, who is incomprehensible:[140]

a soul must renounce all possession of the memory in order to reach union with God in hope, for if hope is to be centred entirely on God, nothing that is not God should reside in the memory. And we have also given proof that no form, figure, image, or idea (whether heavenly or earthly, natural or supernatural) that can be grasped by the memory is God or like to him.[141]

Hope: the green tunic

Hope enables the person to rise above the attractions of the world and the temptations of the devil. Once the person's eyes are fixed on a goal beyond the reach of the world, the self and the devil, and they are filled with the hope of attaining it through the mercy of God, it is easy for them to forgo any temptations that come, especially those of the world. It is unrelenting hope that impels the person to turn their back on the alluring invitations of the world. Thus without hope it would be very difficult to advance on the path of *nada*. The green livery of hope enables the person to walk without any possessions or support in the dark and secret night:[142]

> Over this white tunic of faith the soul puts on a second coloured garment, a green coat of mail. Green, as we said, signifies the virtue of hope, by which one in the first place is defended from the second enemy, the world. This green of living hope in God imparts such courage and valour and so elevates the soul to the things of eternal life that in comparison with these heavenly hopes all earthly things seem, as they truly are, dry, dead, and worthless.[143]

Hope generates a spiritual poverty that leaves the memory free and disencumbered from the past and from the self, leading to self-forgetfulness.[144] Even former favours received are forgotten, in order to maintain spiritual freedom.[145] Hope allows the memory to let go all the heart's possessions of past days, hoping only for eternal life. The only concession John gives in this regard is the retention of certain "images or apprehensions caused by love in order to set the spirit on its course of love".[146] In such a case, the memory is not trapped within the limits of personal history, but has attained its proper function of growth and self-transcendence:[147]

> The soul is thus divested of all worldly garments and does not set her heart on anything there is, or will be, in the world; she lives clothed only in the hope of eternal life. Having her heart so lifted up above the things of the world, she is not only unable to touch or take hold of the worldly things, but she cannot see them.[148]

The tricks and traps of the memory

John warns us that a failure to darken the memory with regard to knowledge and discursive reflection, lays the person open to many types of harm inflicted by the world and the devil.[149] This pair will utilise the treasured possessions of the memory as a bait to play tricks and set traps on the person's path. The memories of bodily experiences will cause them to be prey to many weaknesses like deceptions, imperfections, desires, anxiety, suspicion, inclination to criticise, waste of time, pride, avarice, envy, wrath, and the like. Furthermore, the person's attachment to the contents of the memory deprives them of their ability to turn towards the immutable and incomprehensible God.[150] Even the memories of spiritual or supernatural experiences that we retain constitute a potential threat to our progress. The first kind of harm arises from the fact that our assessment of these experiences is frequently mistaken, we come to believe that a mere figment of the imagination is a revelation from God. The second kind of harm that results is the danger of falling into presumption (in which the person hopes to save themselves either through total reliance on their own capacities, or an 'unengaged' belief in God's mercy which in reality seeks to avoid conversion) and vanity. A third kind derives from the opportunity we give to the 'evil one' to deceive us through our toying with these memories. The fourth harm is the hindrance that is caused by the memory to the attempt to reach union with God in hope, where the hope is entirely centred on God. Finally, the mental perceptions regarding God retained in the memory make the incomprehensible God who is beyond all limits, a 'limited God', who can be contained; this, according to John, is a blasphemous, base, and improper judgement about God. Because of all these evils, memories, even those concerning the experiences received from God, become snares and delusions that lead to sin. We must let go, therefore, of all memories regarding bodily and supernatural experiences, and keep the memory in the darkness of *nada* which encourages the practice of hope. Peter Bourne, while reflecting on the experiences of the dark night, describes humorously the condition of a person who lives in their memories:

> Memories are often binding and blinding. They direct our lives even beyond our will and conscious control. Some persons live on their memories; they will continually talk about themselves, and what *they* experienced, and *they* said, and *they* want, and what *they* like. Try to head them off, by interjecting your own experience, and you will see their enthusiasm wane, only to wait for another chance to blab about *their* life. Usually you will find that they will begin to repeat themselves; they are stuck on certain past injuries or past experiences (the good old days!). What would be your advice to them? Most likely you would tell them to forget it! And that is what John is telling us. Forget the past, it's gone![151]

As mentioned earlier, possession and retention are the natural powers possessed by the memory, which are rather passive acts. The virtue of hope, on the other hand, reshapes the memory giving it the active power of dispossession and forgetfulness, which can generate the required spiritual emptiness.[152] The reason for embarking upon such a programme of negation is the inability of the memory to possess God. Union with God, which is by nature incomprehensible, cannot be reached unless the memory rises above itself.[153] John writes:

> none of the supernatural forms and ideas that can be received by the memory is God. Consequently the memory must likewise dismiss all these forms and ideas in order to reach union with God in hope. Every possession is against hope. As St Paul says, *hope is for what is not possessed* (Rom 8:24).[154]

Advantages of vacating the memory

Until now we have considered the necessity of emptying the memory and the disadvantages that stem from a memory crowded with ideas and images. The advantages of emptying the memory correspond to the disadvantages of a congested memory. The quiet and the peace produced by voiding the memory are increased because the person is now delivered from scrutinising the origin and veracity of supernatural communications. Once the memory is convinced of the worthlessness of its acquisitions and made to renounce those understandings which do not help the person, it turns to hope. Once the barriers erected by our knowledge and memories are dismantled, the "supreme hope in the incomprehensible God"[155] emerges, "as there is no form and no image by which the memory could grasp God".[156] And thus the memory becomes "formless and imageless; the imagination is no longer active, the memory is completely concentrated on the highest good in perfect oblivion, without the slightest remembrance of anything".[157]

As the person learns to detach themselves from all memories, both good and bad, by means of the theological virtue of hope, they obtain the state of poverty of the spirit. Hope is very effective in attaining detachment of the spirit. John is in full agreement with Thomas Aquinas who states, "To him who longs for something great, all lesser things seem small."[158] Absolute trust and full confidence in God enable the person to move forward, even though the future is obscure and dark. Hope purifies the memory of its worldly and, especially, of its spiritual possessions. As long as the person holds on to any perceptions of God obtained through prayer, visions or any other means, they think less of God than they ought and receive less from God. Any target we set ourselves that is based on past experience, brings God down to the level of our own imagination and so takes us from the right path. An active memory destroys the tranquillity and peace of the soul, which are the essential conditions for contemplation. Memory is the ultimate cause of anything that disturbs this peace of soul. A memory emptied of its possessions leads to the experience of *nada* in its fullness. John invites us to leave behind the past and reorient the memory to God so that our past experiences may not play tricks on us and hold us back from progressing towards the true experience of God. John's teaching on memory is based on the promise of God, that is, on God's fidelity to his word manifested to us in Christ:[159]

> What souls must do in order to live in perfect and pure hope in God is this: As often as distinct ideas, forms, and images occur to them, they should immediately, without resting in them, turn to God in loving affection, in emptiness of everything rememberable.[160]

The big objection often raised against the total evacuation of memory is the loss of 'holy' thoughts stored up in the memory. The answer John gives to this objection is that in the state of contemplation such storage does not serve any purpose as it did in the days of meditation:[161] "Contemplation does not require much thinking but much loving."[162] So, as the person passes on to the advanced state of contemplation, words and thoughts become a hindrance rather than a help:

> imagining Christ crucified or at the pillar or in some other scene; or God seated on a throne with resplendent majesty; or

imagining or considering glory as a beautiful light, and so on; or, in similar fashion, any other human or divine object imaginable. The soul will have to empty itself of these images and leave this sense in darkness if it is to reach divine union. For these images, just as the corporeal objects of the exterior senses, cannot be an adequate, proximate means to God.[163]

Charity

Charity, or love, is the virtue that transforms the faculty of the will, purifying it and making it ready for union with God. The will is the protector of the self. In any choice the will puts the interests of the self first; but, to love God means to put him first, in all choices. What results is a tug-of-war between the self and God. The self has its own priorities; its joys and fears. It is the will that directs all our conscious actions, and is itself directed by our feelings and passions. By emptying the will of all selfishness by means of charity, it can be cleansed for the reception of God's will. As noted earlier, John identifies joy, hope, sorrow and fear as the four basic emotions or passions that influence and control the will. Joy can be identified with the pleasure principle and sorrow with the pain principle of modern psychology. 'Hope' in this context is the longing for pleasure, and 'fear' the anxiety over the termination of pleasure and the inception of pain. If self-love, the motivating factor behind these four passions, is intercepted by charity, these longings and anxieties can be transformed. Like joy, the other three passions too have their own role in tormenting the person when they are in control of their will.

As we have seen, the actions of the self are controlled by the will, and the will is apt to be controlled by passions. If the passions, however, are under control, the self is less ready to be commanded by the will; if the self is negated, the passions lose their control over the will: but this control and this negation are impossible for normal human beings without the introduction of a greater force – love for God.[164] By detaching the self from its four basic passions, the individual is raised to a state of freedom which a person oppressed by passions could never dream of. Detachment offers a person great objectivity in judgements. Detachment leaves the heart free to make the right choice – God. Just as faith removes all the barriers erected by human knowledge, and hope removes the oppression caused by possessions, charity – God's love – removes all other types of love that obstruct the person's path to divine union:

> And more intense enkindling of another, better love (love of the soul's Bridegroom) is necessary for the vanquishing of the appetites and the denial of this pleasure. By finding satisfaction and strength in this love, it will have the courage and constancy to readily deny all other appetites. The love of its Bridegroom is not the only requisite for conquering the strength of the sensitive appetites; an enkindling with urgent longings of love is also necessary. For the sensory appetites are moved and attracted towards sensory objects with such cravings that if the spiritual part of the soul is not fired with other, more urgent longings for spiritual things, the soul will be able neither to overcome the yoke of the nature nor to enter the night of sense; nor will it have the courage to live in the darkness of all things by denying its appetites for them.[165]

Our own will is our separation from God. All the disorder, corruption and maladies in our nature lie in the fixation of our will, imagination and desire. This fixation leads us to a state in which we live for ourselves, are our own centre and circumference and act wholly from ourselves according to our own will, imagination and desires. The stripping of the 'I', together with its other forms 'me', and 'mine', that is, a radical abandonment of self to God, is the necessary condition for union with him. In this process, the self will find its position in the mystical body of God and it will humbly take its place in the communal life of reality. The life of union is not a self-loss in an essence, but a self-discovery and self-fulfilment in the union of the heart and will.

The negation of the will means nothing but its consecration to God through love. The process of purifying the will of its various appetites does not mean the suppression of all the natural drives and tendencies. It is liberating the will from its slavery to the oppressing appetites and unruly desires. Temporal goods such as riches, dignity, children and relatives; natural goods such as beauty, intelligence and talent; sensory goods which are brought in through the five senses and imagination; moral goods such as virtues and observance of the law; and supernatural goods such as gift of prophecy, miracles and healing, and so on – all these attract and often enslave the will by urging it to acquire them. Even if some of these goods come directly from God, our voluntary acceptance and desire for them will lead us astray, or at least retard our progress to God. Any desire that fails to direct us to God is enslaving: it must be rejected and the will should be filled with love and desire for God alone. John insists that God should not be sought for, desired or loved for any reason other than his own 'self'.[166]

The will, as the human person's 'control centre', and centre of decision-making and action, is seen by John as the faculty upon which the grace of God acts to develop within us the virtue of love.[167] The content of God's will is summed up in love, for God is love. The human will, therefore, is called to respond to love with love. God's will is that we align our will to his will in love. In a way, love is unique; it differs from faith and hope, for their nature appears to be entirely self-transcending, while love includes within itself elements of genuine attainment and rest. The quality of hope's self-emptying can be judged by the 'possession' of the love of God. The only thing that survives the ruthless *apophatic* denial worked by faith and hope, is love to which faith and hope minister, and which in its turn preserves and animates them. Hence the advice of John is to cast the self upon God in a fine outpouring of love. If not successful in this, the person should make use

of all the spiritual means within their grasp, such as
meditation, interior exercise, and fervent prayer, because,
as Thomas Merton said, summarising his reflections on
John's teachings, "the most important element in the
contemplative life is love".[168] To love unselfishly, an attitude
of detachment is essential. Faith and hope, by themselves,
cannot carry us to full union with God. Full union is a
union of love:[169]

> The strength of the soul comprises the faculties, passions, and
> appetites. All this strength is ruled by the will. When the will
> directs these faculties, passions, and appetites towards God,
> turning away from all that is not God, the soul preserves its
> strength for God, and comes to love him with all its might.[170]

Charity: the red toga

The natural effect of an intense love is self-forgetfulness
and readiness for self-sacrifice.[171] The person absorbed in
God's love is like a martyr who eagerly opts for self-
sacrifice. For this reason John compares love to a red
garment, a toga. What takes place on the path of *nada* is a
dynamic Easter transformation.[172] When two wills are in
complete conformity, so that there is nothing in the one
that is displeasing to the other, a union is effected.[173] A
person who has made great progress in intimacy with God
sees everything in relation to him.[174] At this point God's
love transfigures them and makes them the limpid medium
in which God is known.[175] The splendid scarlet garment
stands not only for the person's active love "for God's
sake",[176] but also for God's "strong love"[177] towards the
person. This 'strong love' of God is often felt by the person
as if "all the rivers of the world are coming upon them and
assailing them, and they feel that all their previous actions
and passions are overwhelmed by it".[178] To be subjected to
this love is, in a sense, a passive experience and it imparts a
feeling of being 'wrapped up'. John explains:

Over the white and green (vestments)... the soul puts on a third colour, a precious red toga. This colour denotes charity... (which gives) protection and concealment from the flesh, her third enemy. For where there is true love of God, love of self and one's own things find no entry. Not only does charity protect her, but it even makes the other virtues genuine, strengthens and invigorates them in order to fortify the soul, and bestows on them loveliness and charm so as to please the Beloved thereby.[179]

A charity that has any ulterior motivations is not pure. A person who remains prone to selfish enjoyments and the things of this world will not be ready to identify themselves with God. Real charity blossoms only out of a heart empty of self. The compassion of such a heart towards a suffering brother or sister is not the result of its 'other-centeredness' but its selflessness. The action of a person who has encountered *nada* is not oppressive but liberating, they never take pride in their achievements. John holds together these two aspects of love which strengthen the soul for "the perfect union of the love of God".[180] In order to save anyone on the true spiritual path from the pitfalls of an egoistic, heroic service, John offers the following warning:

Yet once she (the soul) arrives, she should not become involved in other works and exterior exercises that might be of the slightest hindrance to the attentiveness of love towards God, even though the work is of great service to God. For a little of this pure love is more precious to God and the soul and more beneficial to the Church, even though it seems one is doing nothing, than all these other works put together... Great wrong would be done to a soul who possesses some degree of this solitary love, as well as to the Church, if we were to urge her to become occupied in exterior or active things, even if the works were very important and required for only a short time... After all, this love is the end for which we were created... Let those, then, who are singularly active, who think they can win the world with their preaching and exterior works, observe here that they would profit the Church and please God much more... (and) they would then certainly accomplish more, and with less labour, by one work, than they otherwise would by a thousand... Without prayer they would do a great deal of hammering but accomplish little, and sometimes nothing, and even at times cause harm... However much they may appear to achieve externally, they will in substance be accomplishing nothing.[181]

Various types of love

On certain occasions, Christian love can be measured by its object. Thus it is clear that love of neighbour takes precedence over self-love, and love of God over both. But Christian love can be measured more fruitfully by the nature of the love itself than by its object, given that it is directed ultimately to God in all cases. For John charity does not include a possessive desire for any created things including human relationships, for with such desires, we necessarily love God less, wanting something in addition to him for our happiness. Like Paul, who lists the qualities of real love (1 Cor 13:1-8), John, in his *Flame*, talks of three "qualities of excellence" in the love for God found in someone who has surrendered totally to him,[182] the essence of which is selflessness. Love can be broadly divided into two types: possessive and non-possessive, that is, selfish and unselfish. The demand of Jesus to hate father and mother in order to be true disciples (Lk 14:26) is to be understood in this way, because children love their parents with possessiveness. There is a certain amount of selfishness in that love. For a child to be deprived of the possession of this love and to let go of their possessive attachment to it, amounts to hating it. If the desire for possession still persists, even in the absence of the object, the attachment remains. Detachment is impossible until the child starts hating its possession. Once the attachment and the possessive attitude are overcome, it is possible to turn back to the same old possession with a different attitude – a non-possessive love or admiration. This second kind of love is qualitatively different from the first. In order to love a parent with a true love, first must come detachment: 'hating' them. This experience is often painful to both parties, because such an attachment is natural and gives great comfort. But to enter the world of selfless, non-possessive love one has to detach oneself from all possessive bonds. Not only parent-child relationships, but in every relationship where elements of possessive love can be traced, there is the need to say 'goodbye'. Much of what we call 'love', in fact, is not love, but possessiveness. Jesus has demonstrated to us how God's love operates through his words and deeds.

For John the human person's ultimate happiness is to be found not in creatures but in God, in whom lies every good. God would not be perfect and infinite if he could not satisfy humankind's desire for happiness. In this life, of course, we do not possess God fully, and so it is often held that we need created things too. Even while acknowledging the complementarity of and the need of rapport between creatures, John insists that, in all the stages of spiritual growth, God is ultimately the source of authentic happiness. Only by being united in love with God, and desiring nothing more than doing his will, can one be happy in this life and in the life hereafter.[183] When we long for pleasant relations with others, our love is selfish. What we are searching for in such a case is our comfort and pleasure. Selfless love desires nothing in return. It is not hard to understand how desire for things like relationships and considerate treatment from others can undermine love. In the twentieth chapter of the third book of *Ascent* John clearly describes the method to cultivate friendships through our actions while not desiring them, but actually enjoying them even more than ever before.[184] For John detachment is not only compatible with love of neighbour, but essential. Charity and *agape*, involve loving others for the sake of God, desiring nothing in return. As we begin to realise that our love of the other springs not from the quality of the other, but from their being from God, the focus of our love changes. With such a transformed state of mind we can appreciate everything, and we are attracted to everything: we no longer consider the other from the point of view of their usefulness or their charm. There is no preference, everything is welcome in as much as it comes from God and shines with the glory of God.

A preferential love generally results in a lack of esteem for those who are devoid of the qualities that are prized. A preferential love for God, however, embraces every bit of creation since he is the author and preserver of it. Possessive love, or *eros*, idolises the preferred persons or things because of their beauty, talent, or other such qualities and neglects the downtrodden and unattractive. John was clear on the many vices resulting from such love, which is blind, egoistic, demanding, and enslaving. Such love gets tired of things and persons sooner or later when the novelty is lost or better options are in view. A non-possessive love is a trait of maturity; it neither abandons nor is afraid of abandonment; it always rests in peace. Detached love enables a person to enjoy friendships fully and to express themselves without fear. In detached love there is no unnatural repression of natural human desires.[185]

John stresses that charity empties the will of all its desires.[186] This stripping of the desires for God is an act of love for God, whereby the person totally gives themselves to God. Just as an act of detachment is an act of love, the habit of detachment is the habit of love. It may be hard to grasp the fact that detachment for God is love, because there is a tendency to think of love in terms of good feelings. People can empty themselves of desires for created things through love. John explains this dynamic as follows: just as the appetites weaken the desire to be virtuous, the desire to be virtuous weakens the desires for created things. If we feed our desire to love, we mortify our other desires. The desire to love displaces all other desires of an enlightened soul. If we channel more energy into the desire to love, there may be less fuel for our other fancies. John stresses that it is the love for God that plunges the soul into the dark night. He begins his poem 'Dark Night' with the verse, "One dark night, fired with love's urgent longings", and explains that here the soul "departed on a dark night, attracted by God and enkindled with love for Him alone".[187] John further clarifies:

> The more people rejoice over something outside God, the less intense will be their joy in God; and the more their hopes go out towards something else, the less there is of it for God; and so on with the others... The entire matter of reaching union with God consists in purging the will of its appetites and emotions so that from a human and lowly will it may be changed into the Divine Will, made identical with the will of God.[188]

Even though John saw love as an operation of the will, for him the love or compassion that emerges from the heart of the person immersed in *nada* is not just a voluntary or free act of the will. It is a passive love that flows naturally from the very nature of the person. This is important, and might seem surprising in the light of what we have been saying up to now. This passive love does not act upon the will directly because the will is free, and this burning love is more a passion of love than a free act of the will. The warmth of love wounds the substance of the soul and thus moves the affections passively. John calls this enkindling of love, the "passion of love".[189]

Charity: a drive towards *nada*

Nada brings us face to face with God since it is our passion of love for God that enables us to enter a total detachment from everything else. It is fitting and reasonable, though not strictly necessary, that God should love us in return. Jesus has promised us saying, "If anyone loves me, he will keep my word, and my Father will love him, and we will come to him and make our abode with him" (Jn 14:23).

God's freedom is not restricted by this promise, for God freely chose to make the promise. John sees an integral relationship between our self-emptying love and God's infused love.[190] He declares even more boldly that the extent of our transformation in God depends upon our self-emptying love, and not upon God's love: "The extent of illumination is not dependent upon the ray of sunlight but upon the window. If the window is totally clean and pure, the sunlight will so transform and illumine it."[191] For John, while it is true that God must place the person in the supernatural state of union, "an individual must insofar as possible prepare himself. This he can do naturally with God's help. In the measure that he embarks through his own efforts upon this negation and emptiness of forms, he will receive from God the possession of union."[192] John says that our self-emptying love can even merit God's love.[193]

For John, even consolations that come from God, like the gifts of wisdom, healing, and prophecy, do not unite us with God, for they are not God himself; we are to be united to God, not his gifts, which can be bestowed upon the worst sinners without necessarily transforming them.[194] A 'living death', or a spiritual gift of ourselves in self-emptying faith, hope, and charity, unites us with God without the necessity of extraordinary consolations. John affirms that charity not only prepares the person for union with God but is also the means suitable for effecting that union:[195] "Charity also empties and annihilates the affections and appetites of the will of whatever is not God and centres them on him alone. Thus charity prepares the will and unites it with God through love."[196] John describes the union with God through love in the spiritual marriage in terms of perfect conformity to God's will in charity.

The goal of spiritual life, then, is the complete offering of the self to God through faith, hope, and charity in imitation of Christ on the cross. When the soul is reduced to nothing, spiritual union will be effected between the person and God.[197] Spiritual progress should be measured, John insists, not by divine consolations passively received without the free consent of the will, but by charity and all the virtues actively cultivated, so that union with God and the greatness of the work accomplished will be measured by the person's annihilation for God in the sensory and spiritual parts, in other words, by their detachment. This detachment is for God alone, that is, for doing God's will by loving. The person increases in the love of God as they progress in detachment. Love is the consummation of the spiritual life.[198]

The role of God in the self-emptying process

John often speaks of spiritual exercises in terms of tearing down rather than building up.[199] According to him, progress in contemplation and in union to God are fully dependent on God's will. All the exercising of our senses and faculties that we do must consequently be left behind and silenced, so that God may unite himself to the person. The process of disencumbering, emptying and depriving the faculties of their natural authority and way of operating makes room for the inflow and illumination of the supernatural.[200] Even the renunciation that brings freedom cannot be attained through our own effort. It is a 'sheer grace' to be released from the prison of the self without hindrance from the 'jailers'. Through original sin (our congenital involvement in the sin of the world[201]), says John, the person is held is a captive, subject to passions and natural appetites. When liberated from this bondage and submission, they consider their escape in which they are unnoticed and unimpeded by their passions and appetites, a sheer grace:

> The soul, then, should advert that God is the principal agent in this matter... It should use all its principal care in watching so

as not to place any obstacle in the way of God, its guide on this way ordained for it by Him according to the perfection of His law and of the faith.[202]

This escape refers to the two ways of searching after God: one consists in a departure from all things, effected through a deeply-felt turning away from them; the other is a process of going out from ourselves through self-forgetfulness, which is achieved by the love of God. It is possible to practise *nada* in a proud and self-centred way through ascetical practices. In such cases, the person compromises *nada* practice by pride in their achievements and needs to undergo further *kenotic* purification by God's grace. When the grace of God touches the person, it so raises them up that it not only impels them to go out from self in forgetfulness, but draws them away from things that naturally gave them support, from their habitual way of acting and inclinations, thus inducing them to cast themselves upon God.[203] To those who undergo this frightful experience, John has some words of consolation:

> Oh, then, spiritual soul, when you see your appetites darkened, your inclinations dry and constrained, your faculties incapacitated for any interior exercise, do not be afflicted; think of this as a grace, since God is freeing you from yourself and taking from you your own activity... God takes you by the hand and guides you in darkness, as though you were blind, along a way and to a place you know not. You would never have succeeded in reaching this place no matter how good your eyes and your feet.[204]

We have already seen how John compares the various faculties operating in our body, and the passions and appetites they generate, to the members of a household. When awake, they will permit neither outsiders to enter the house nor the person to go out to meet their beloved. What is more, all our natural abilities are insufficient to put these householders to sleep. Therefore, John says, "It was sheer grace for this soul that God in this night put to sleep all the members of the household".[205] Yet, when a person is elevated to the level of total renunciation, they know themselves to be in possession of all:

> Mine are the heavens and mine is the earth. Mine are the nations, the just are mine, and mine the sinners. The angels are mine, and the mother of God, and all things are mine; and God himself is mine and for me, because Christ is mine and all for me. Why do you ask, then, and seek my soul? Yours is all of this, and all is for you. Do not engage yourself in something less or pay heed to the crumbs that fall from your father's table. Go forth and exult in your glory! Hide yourself in it and rejoice, and you will obtain the supplications of your soul.[206]

God in search of love

The insistence on the need of personal efforts for the attainment of *nada* might leave us with the erroneous impression that the person anxiously searches after a God who plays 'hide and seek' with them. This is not the case: John points out that it is God who continuously seeks us and it is we who keep hiding from him.[207] God loved us first (1 Jn 4:19) and extended his helping hand to make us be like him (1 Jn 3:2). John expresses the desperate need of God's assistance in our progress to him in the following prayer:

> Who can free themselves from lowly manners and limitations if you do not lift them to yourself, my God, in purity of love? How will human beings begotten and nurtured in lowliness rise up to you, Lord, if you do not raise them with your hand that made them?[208]

The bride's absconding from her house, was made possible only because there was a 'gravitational pull' arising from God, who was constantly acting within her. The good news according to John is this: "it should be known that if anyone is seeking God, the Beloved is seeking that person much more."[209] While John insists on the total gratuitous nature of union with God, due to his confidence in the benevolence of God, he is also positive regarding the coming of God into a person who has entered *nada*:

> As the sun rises in the morning and shines on your house so that its light may enter if you open the shutters, so God, who in watching over Israel does not doze (Ps.121:4) or, still less, sleep, will enter the soul that is empty, and fill it with divine goods.[210]

Three signs to stop meditation

Even though the role alloted to the person in the process of self-emptying is secondary to that of their divine counterpart, and the longing of the divine lover for union with his loved one far exceeds that of his bride, any premature slackening of the effort to attain *el todo* will inevitably retard their spiritual progress. To continue the struggle beyond a certain point, on the other hand, especially in meditation, is not only wearisome but also detrimental to the same progress. To clear any confusion, therefore, John offers three signs which indicate when the time to stop meditation has come. The first sign is the absence of the benefits usually derived from the exercise of the faculty of imagination in meditation, and the person now suffers from dryness and boredom, and meditation becomes wearisome. The second sign is the person's inability to focus their imagination on anything in particular. Imaginative representations become vague and confusing, and they simply have no wish to use their imagination. The third sign – which John calls the surest sign – is the desire to love God in quiet, without imagining anything and without seeking consolations.

As the person advances still further, even this desire to love God in quiet will be withdrawn so that they may experience the total darkness of abandonment which Jesus experienced on the cross during the last moments of his earthly life. This crucial moment of 'divine rejection' can be survived only through a total self-negation, saying: 'Your will be done'. This is the fateful moment in which the self dies. The person who survives this decisive experience of *nada* will not be touched by any spirit other than that of God and will function as an instrument in the hands of God:

> It is manifestly a great grace for the soul to have successfully undertaken this departure, in which she liberated herself from the devil, the world, and her own sensuality. In having reached the happy freedom of the spirit desired by all, the soul went from the lowly to the sublime; being earthly she became heavenly; and being human she became divine.[211]

Active passivity

It is true that while discussing the 'active dark night' John vehemently insists on the role of human action. In the first book of *Ascent* he even gives us a detailed list of "inclinations"[212] one has to develop in order to progress on the path to perfection, yet he considers these activities an expression of the human good will in response to the invitation of God's grace towards greater perfection. He warns the practitioner that all the ascetical feats undertaken with a view to attain *nada* or enter union with God will ultimately prove futile. In the final analysis, *nada* is the result of God's intervention in the life of an individual:

> Yet until a soul is placed by God in the passive purgation of that dark night, which we will soon explain, it cannot purify itself completely of these imperfections or others. But people should insofar as possible strive to do their part of purifying and perfecting themselves and thereby merit God's divine cure. In this cure God will heal them of what through their own efforts they were unable to remedy. No matter how much individuals do through their own efforts, they cannot actively

purify themselves enough to be disposed in the least degree for the divine union of the perfection of love. God must take over and purge them in that fire that is dark for them.[213]

John attributes the experience of *nada* to the purifying action of the Spirit, and as a sign of the unintelligible activity of God taking place in the person's innermost core. When the person, with a sense of total trust, abandons themselves to God's providence, the Spirit takes charge of them. The person in such a state, however, will not be aware of the changes that are taking place within them: a sense of abandonment, desolation and darkness often overtakes and torments them. Any active effort to save themselves from this pitiable state will only block the Spirit's work of transformation of the individual:

> Individuals should take note that, even though they do not seem to be making any progress in this quietude or doing anything, they are advancing much faster than if they were treading alone on foot, for God is carrying them. Although they are walking at God's pace, they do not feel this pace. Even though they do not work with their faculties, they achieve much more than if they did, for God is the agent... A soul, then, should abandon itself into God's hands, and not into its own or those of the other two blind guides. Insofar as it abandons itself to God and does not apply its faculties to anything, it will advance securely.[214]

The state of *nada* is an experience that is to be accepted and sustained willingly because God accomplishes great things in this nothingness. John insists, "Do not say, therefore: 'The soul does not advance, because it is not doing anything'. For it is true that it is not doing anything, I will prove to you that it is accomplishing a great deal by doing nothing".[215] He goes on to describe what is 'achieved' during the passivity of a resolute person. The unbridled faculties, one by one, are brought under control and are kept under the command of reason. Reason, in its turn, is no longer fed by natural human intelligence, but by the Spirit:

First, the Bridegroom conjures and commands the useless wanderings of the phantasy and imaginative power to cease once and for all. He also puts under the control of reason the two natural powers, the irascible and the concupiscible which were previously somewhat of an affliction to the soul. And, insofar as is possible in this life, he perfects the three faculties (memory, intellect, and will) in regard to their objects. What is more, he conjures and commands the four passions (joy, hope, fear, and sorrow). So from now on they will be mitigated and controlled by reason.[216]

Conclusion

Our examination of the progressive steps of *nada* according to John of the Cross reveals the presence of two convergent perspectives. From the human point of view it is a path of deliberate action, while from a supernatural perspective the person is simply receptive or passive to God's initiative. Until the person loses their appetite for things, they are not ready to start their journey towards their beloved; as long as the householders and the guards are awake and the person is under their protection, they cannot bring the beloved in or go out in search of him; yet to get them to fall sleep is beyond the person's capability. Without the sheer grace given by the beloved, escape is impossible. It is in fact the veiled presence of the beloved and his knock on the door that wake them up and enkindle their heart with 'love's urgent longings'. Thus John emphasises how utterly powerless we are to bring about the union on our own and insists on the futility of all self-induced renunciation. Furthermore, and importantly, John insists that it is not we who are the seeker but rather God who is in search of his 'lost love'. To unify these two different aspects of the spiritual drama, that is, the role of both human and divine action, John uses a concept of 'active passivity', or positive availability. What God requires of us is not initiative but co-operation. We must withdraw from other lovers, vacate and decorate the bridal chamber, keep watch and open up at the first knock on the door.

Seen from the human point of view the path of spiritual progress mapped out by John is a call to self-surrender through renunciation. Renunciation is a waiting for God. It is constant wakefulness, watchfulness and availability. Renunciation is not a negative term in John's spirituality: it is being free for God. Renunciation is the product of love, and its goal is love. In other words, renunciation is *of* lovers, initiated *by* lovers and is undertaken *for* the sake of the loved one. Renunciation for any other motive is not acceptable to John. Evangelical counsels and theological virtues are for John the means to empty oneself to bring about an attitude of receptivity to the downpouring of God's grace. The practice of the evangelical counsels – chastity, obedience and poverty – prepares and strengthens the person to walk on the path of *nada*. Chastity tames the flesh, while obedience drives away the devil and poverty triumphs over the world. These preliminary steps culminate in the theological virtues – faith, hope and charity – which become so perfect that they blend together to give rise to a harmonious experience of love. The veil of faith becomes so thin that through it the person obtains a real foretaste of the vision of God. Hope becomes so real that the person has the feeling of already possessing what they hope for. Both these virtues intensify the person's love and in turn become overshadowed by it. Faith causes emptiness in the intellect with respect to understanding; the intellect which is reduced to nothingness gives way to the obscure knowledge of faith. Hope causes emptiness in memory with regard to all possessions; it empties the memory to such an extent that there remains no trace of past experiences, only a hope for the things which are not yet possessed (Rom 8:24). Charity causes emptiness in the will through detachment from affections in all that is not God; it frees the will from all things by dispossessing them. The result of all this is an emptiness which allows God to unite himself with the person. John tells us, "To arrive at being all, desire to be nothing. To come to the knowledge of all, desire the knowledge of nothing".[217] This way of total renunciation is the narrow way, found by very few:

> The soul must ordinarily walk this path to reach that sublime and joyous union with God. Recognising the narrowness of the path and the fact that so very few tread it – as the Lord himself says (Mt 7, 14) – the soul's song in this first stanza is one of happiness in having advanced along it to this perfection of love. Appropriately, this constricted road is called a dark night.[218]

At the heart of John's teaching is the message of the mystics of all times: in God alone lies human fulfilment. For John it is love that unites us with God. The greater the degree of love we have, the greater the profundity with which we are united with God. These are the many mansions of which Jesus said, "In my Father's house are many mansions"(Jn 14:2). In order for us to maintain our progress, we reach the innermost centre of God[219] and "get lost in his love".[220] John proposes only one way: total renunciation and self-surrender, "keeping nothing back for herself".[221] That is precisely the reason why Pope John Paul II calls John the "Master in the Faith", and why John is universally recognised as towering personality in the field of mysticism.[222]

NOTES

1 *2A* 5,4.
2 *LF* 2,27.
3 *LF* 2,27.
4 Cf. *Catechism of the Catholic Church*, (London: Geoffrey Chapman, 1994), paragraphs 1854-1861.
5 *1N* 12,2.
6 *C* 1,1.
7 *2N* 24,4.
8 Seemingly complex, this analysis is essentially simple: human beings function on the level of sense, and spirit. Cf. I. Matthew, OCD, *The Impact of God: Soundings from St John of the Cross* (London: Hodder and Stoughton, 1995), 59.

9   *2A* 2,2. Cf. *Catechism of the Catholic Church*, paragraphs 362-368. The
     Catechism offers, amongst others, this definition of the soul: "The
     innermost aspect of man, that which is of greatest value in him, that by
     which he is most especially in God's image".
10   *2A* 16,2.
11   D.B. Tillyer, *Union with God*, 38-46.
12   *1N* 4,2; *2N* 16,4; *LF* 3,34.
13   *3A* 16,2; *2A* 6,2; *2A* 6,6; *2N* 21,11.
14   *2A* 5,8.
15   *C* 1,3.
16   *2A* 12,2; 16,2-3; 17,4; *C* 18,7.
17   *3A* 16,6.
18   D.B. Tillyer, *Union with God*, 51-52.
19   *1A* 6,6-7.
20   *1A* 11,2.
21   D.B. Tillyer, *Union with God*, 56.
22   *2A* 7,5.
23   *1A* 5,6.
24   *1A* 13,6.
25   *Prec* 1.
26   *C* 3,7.
27   *LF* 3, 65.
28   *1N* 6,2.
29   *1A* 3,4.
30   *2N* 23,13.
31   *2N* 24,2.
32   *2N* 24,3.
33   E. Underhill, *Mysticism*, 223.
34   *1A* 2,1.
35   *LF* 1,19-22.
36   R. Collings, *John of the Cross*, 95.
37   *Ibid*.
38   'Dark Night', Stanzas 1 & 2.
39   *A* Prologue, 9.
40   *A* Prologue, 8.
41   E. Stein, *The Science of the Cross*, 31.
42   *Catechism of the Catholic Church*, paragraphs 915, 1973-4.
43   *3A* 23,3.
44   *Prec.* 4-17.
45   *C* 3,5.
46   *1A* 8,4.
47   *A* Prologue, 9.
48   *Catechism of the Catholic Church*, paragraphs 2518ff.
49   E. Underhill, *Mysticism*, 205.
50   E. Underhill, *Mysticism*, 205.
51   Purity of heart – *Sayings* 173; *3A* 26,6; 35,7; 36,1; 45,4; *1N* 6,4; *2N*
     12,1. Purity of soul – *Sayings* 49; *2A* 15,4; 24,6; *3A* 3,4; 23,4; 26,7;

1N 6,1; 13,6; *2N* 9,1; *C* 20-21,2; 27,6; 34,2; *LF* 1,9; 1,17; 2,17; 2,19; 2,24; 3,24; 4,14.

52 *C* 27,6-8.

53 *Catechism of the Catholic Church*, paragraph 2347.

54 *Catechism of the Catholic Church*, paragraph 2395.

55 P.M. Quay, *The Christian Meaning of Human Sexuality* (San Francisco: Ignatius, 1985), 92.

56 *Catechism of the Catholic Church*, paragraph 2394.

57 *C* 30,7.

58 *3A* 27,4; *1N* 2,5.

59 Some of the principal New Testamental references concerning the counsel of celibacy are: Mt 19:8-12 (Not all are called to be celibates); Lk 18:28-30 (Set apart for the Kingdom); Mk 10:28-30 (leave marriage and family for Kingdom in the future and the hundredfold now); Mt 22:30; Mk 12:25 (There is no marriage in heaven); 1 Cor 7:1-9,25-38 (Marriage is better for most Christians. They may abstain from sexual relations with mutual consent periodically for spiritual motives. Those who have a special call may embrace celibacy for the sake of an undivided personal involvement with God).

60 P.M. Conner, *Celibate Love*, 105.

61 *Sayings* 85; 156; *1N* 6,1-2; 12,8; *Prec.* 11-12.

62 *Prec.* 12.

63 T. Spidlík, *The Spirituality*, 283-288.

64 R. Burrows, *Ascent to Love*, 41.

65 *Prec.* 11.

66 S. Walker (ed), *Speaking of Silence: Christians and Buddhists on the Contemplative Way* (New Jersey: Paulist Press, 1987), 27.

67 L. of St Joseph, *The Secret of Sanctity*, 54.

68 *1N* 6,2.

69 L. of St Joseph, *The Secret of Sanctity*, 58.

70 *Letter* 32; N. Cummins, *Freedom to Rejoice*, 44.

71 *Prec.* 11.

72 A. Cugno, *John of the Cross: The Life and Thought of a Christian Mystic* (tr., B. Wall), (London: Burns & Oates, 1982), 42-44.

73 *Letter* 16.

74 *2A* 15,4; 24,8-9; *2N* 6,4-5.

75 *2N* 9,4.

76 *Prec.* 7.

77 S. Muto, *Approaching the Sacred* (New Jersey: Dimension Books, 1973), 126.

78 E. Underhill, *Mysticism*, 211.

79 E. Underhill, *Mysticism*, 208.

80 W. Johnston, *The Mystical Way*, 323.

81 *2A* 7,11.

82 *1A* 3,4.

83 *1A* 3,4.

84 *C* 14-15,5.

85 *Letter* 16.
86 *1A* 1,3.
87 *LF* 3,46.
88 *3A* 20,3.
89 *C* 1.14.
90 *1N* 8,2-3.
91 *1N* 12,2.
92 *2N* 6,5.
93 *Sayings* 174.
94 *2N* 4,1.
95 *2N* 4,1.
96 *2A* 15,4.
97 *C* 10,6.
98 *LF* 3,48; *Letter* 7.
99 *1A* 4,3.
100 *3A* 19,8.
101 *3A* 11,1.
102 *Prec.* 4-17.
103 *3A* 18,8; *3A* 19,5; *2N* 7,4; *2N* 9,1; *1A* 4,6; *C* 35,2-3.
104 *2A* 6,2.
105 *2N* 21,11-12.
106 *1A* 2,1; *2A* 1,1-3,6;
107 *2A* 6,1-3.
108 *2A* 6,4-5.
109 *2N* 6,6.
110 R. Collings, *John of the Cross*, 102.
111 P. Bourne, *John of the Cross and the Dark Night: Understanding His Ascent and Dark Night in Easy Stages* (Long Beach, CA: Wenzel Press, 1993), 46.
112 *2A* 24,8.
113 *2A* 9,1.
114 *2A* 8,6.
115 *2N* 5,3; *C* 15-16,16; *LF* 3,49.
116 *2A* 3,2.
117 *2A* 9,1.
118 H. McCabe, O.P., *The Teaching of the Catholic Church: A New Catechism of Christian Doctrine* (London: Catholic Truth Society, 1985), 14.
119 *2N* 21,3.
120 *2N* 21,3.
121 *2N* 21,4.
122 *2N* 21,4-5.
123 *2A* 8,7.
124 P. John Paul II (K. Wojtyla), "The Question of Faith in John of the Cross", in J. Sullivan (ed.) *Contemporary Psychology*, 240.
125 *Ibid.* 235.
126 *2A* 1,1.

127 *2A* 22,3,5.
128 *2A* 22,7.
129 R. Burrows, *Ascent to Love*, 72.
130 *Collected Works* (Kavanaugh & Rodriguez), pp. 718-19.
131 *2A* 1,3.
132 D. B. Tillyer, *Union with God*, 49.
133 *2A* 1,2.
134 *2A* 12,3.
135 *2A* 4,2.
136 R. Collings, *John of the Cross*, 121.
137 *2A* 6,1-3.
138 *3A* 15,1.
139 *LF* 1,36.
140 D. B. Tillyer, *Union with God*, 49.
141 *3A* 11,1.
142 *2N* 21,8.
143 *2N* 21,6.
144 R. Collings, *John of the Cross*, 128.
145 *3A* 9,4.
146 *3A* 13,6.
147 R. Collings, *John of the Cross*, 130.
148 *2N* 21,6.
149 *3A* 3-5.
150 *3A* 5,3.
151 P. Bourne, *John of the Cross*, 82.
152 R. Collings, *John of the Cross*, 126.
153 *Ibid.* 127.
154 *3A* 7,2.
155 *3A* 2,3.
156 *3A* 2,4.
157 *3A* 2,4.
158 Quoted in N. Cummins, *Freedom to Rejoice*, 107.
159 N. Cummins, *Freedom to Rejoice*, 115.
160 *3A* 15,2.
161 *2A* 12,3.
162 *2A* 12,8.
163 *2A* 12,3.
164 *1A* 14,2.
165 *1A* 14,2.
166 *C* 3,1; 9,7.
167 *2N* 12,6-7; 13,8.
168 T. Merton, *Ascent to Truth*, 274.
169 D. B. Tillyer, *Union with God*, 50.
170 *3A* 16,2.
171 S. M. M. Gabriel, *Spiritual Director according to the principles of John of the Cross* (Cork: The Mercier Press, 1951), 76-79.
172 R. Rolheiser, "John and Human Development", in J. McGowan

(ed), *A fresh approach to John of the Cross* (Middlegreen, Slough: St Pauls, 1993), 35.

173 P. John Paul II (K. Wojtyla), *Faith according to John of the Cross* (San Francisco: Ignatius Press, 1981), 53.

174 S. M. M. Gabriel, *Union with God according to John of the Cross* (Eugene, Oregon: Carmel of Maria Regina, 1990), 79.

175 T. Merton, *Ascent to Truth,* 278.

176 *2A* 5,7.

177 *C* 31,4.

178 *C* 14,9.

179 *2N* 21,10.

180 *2N* 18,4.

181 *C* 29,2-3.

182 *LF* 3,82.

183 *LF* 3,82.

184 *3A* 20,2-3.

185 *3A* 22,2-3.

186 *2A* 2,6,4.

187 *1A* 1,1&4.

188 *3A* 16,2,3.

189 *2N* 13,3.

190 *2A* 5,4.

191 *2A* 5,6.

192 *3A* 2,13.

193 *1N* 3,3.

194 *3A* 30,4.

195 *2A* 6,1.

196 *2N* 21,11.

197 *2A* 7,11.

198 A. Cugno, *John of the Cross,* 63.

199 *3A* 2.1.

200 *3A* 2,2.

201 H. McCabe, O.P., *The Teaching of the Catholic Church,* 12.

202 *LF* 3,29.

203 *C* 1,20.

204 *2N* 16,7.

205 *2N* 14,1.

206 *Sayings* 26.

207 *C* 22,1; *LF* 3,28.

208 *Sayings* 26.

209 *LF* 3,28.

210 *LF* 3,46.

211 *2N* 22,1.

212 *1A* 13,6.

213 *1N* 3,3; cf. *1N* 7,5.

214 *LF* 3,67.

215 *LF* 3,47.

216 *C* 20-21,4.
217 *1A* 13,11.
218 *1N* Prologue.
219 *C* 27,3.
220 *C* 29,7.
221 *C* 27,3.
222 P. Boyce, "The Influence of John of the Cross in Britain and Ireland", *Teresianum* 42/1 (1991), 97.

FOUR

ASPECTS OF *NADA*: THE 'WOMB' OF THE 'AWAKENED SELF'

Introduction

John saw and explored the unlimited potential of *nada*, which is realised only through self-transcendence. He discovered the creative power of God, which emanates from the abyss of *nada*. During the dark nights of his life John came to the awareness that God is present in *nada* and that it is in *nada* that his creative power is fully operational. The law of evolution at work in God's creatures brings about only minute and gradual modifications, while substantial and massive changes occur when creatures made in his image are sent to the abyss of *nada*. *Nada* is not only the tomb but also the womb of creation. *Nada* stands for possibilities, new beginnings and new life.[1] *Nada* is not negative in its essence. It is not an antonym of the word *reality*. Similarly, John's unremitting *via negativa* cannot simply be explained away as being a rejection of any involvement, an involvement by its nature sinful, with creatures. *Nada* is positive. It is the womb of all the positive things we encounter. It is the source and ground of all being. It is the workshop of the Creator. *Nada* means openness, non-resistance, and super-conductivity. *Nada* unfolds possibilities of every sort. God exercises his full creative power in *nada*. God was able to work effectively in the 'beginning' because there was only *nada*, which offered "no resistence."[2] God can work equally effectively in those who embrace *nada* in their life. Such people are like pure air, clear water, or clean glass. They offer no resistance to God's intervention. They transmit God through their words, deeds and existence. It is the 'corrupted self' and its egoism that blemish the person and make them opaque. As far as a person succeeds in overcoming their resistance to God, that is, in surmounting egoism, they become permeated by God through *nada* and start transmitting the indwelling divine light. *Nada* is therefore not the absence of being but a true, concrete living of nothingness. As William Johnston summarises it, "Nothingness is an ocean of incredible wealth, a treasure-house of unearthly beauty."[3]

The progressive ascent through the steps of *nada* enables a person to crucify their ego and to die to everything that is not God. Jesus used the cross for his self-sacrifice and God raised him up. The voluntary embracing of *nada* is the new baptism in the 'dark waters' of faith that washes away all the person's impurities. The old self dies and is buried in the tomb of *nada* and a new self emerges from the womb of *nada*. Only a person thus liberated has the ability to see and enjoy life in its fullness. Just as a blind man never grasps the beauty of a rainbow, or a slave, if satisfied with their daily bread, never conceives the joy of liberty, a person who has never entered *nada*, will never appreciate the experience it offers. John considers the experience of *nada* an awakening to a supernatural way of seeing things. He says, "We then ought to say that in this movement it is the soul that is moved and awakened from the sleep of natural vision to supernatural vision. Hence it very adequately uses the term 'awakening'."[4] The person who emerges from *nada* is struck with wonder by everything they encounter, as if awakening from a deep slumber. Everything seems very different to their eyes even though the things themselves remain the same. The reason John gives for this strange experience is that the person is made a stranger to their usual knowledge and experience of things because of their total detachment. In such a state the person "may be informed with the divine,"[5] since they belong more to the next life rather than this. John further clarifies:

> And here lies the remarkable delight of this awakening: the soul knows creatures through God and not God through creatures. This amounts to knowing the effects through their cause and not the cause through its effects. This latter knowledge is *a posteriori* [where one reasons from particular facts to a general principle], and the former is essential knowledge.[6]

Although John did not treat the concept of *nada* in a systematic way, an analysis of his writings provides us with enough material to understand what he precisely meant by *nada*. His concept of *nada* was not exactly his brainchild, but the outcome of his mystical experience. It is this very same experience that forms the basis for his theological, philosophical and spiritual 'projects'. He makes it clear that his aim in writing was to present a substantial and solid doctrine for those who desire union with God. He marks out a straight and narrow path that begins, continues and ends with *nada* for those who long to reach perfection. Hence we can assume that *nada* is not just a part of his way to perfection, but the axis of his mystical theology. John's entire pedagogical effort was directed towards a single goal: to convince the seeker of the need of experiencing *nada*, the only viable means to reach *el todo*. A total self-emptying is absolutely required for a true awakening to the Absolute.[7] The life of union that is achieved in travelling along the obscure path of *nada* is nothing other than a life of *nada*.

Nada: the 'womb'

The Pauline phrase 'new self' (Eph 4:24; Col 3:10) was a great inspiration to John. We notice this phrase with its various interchangeable terms like 'renewed self', 'spiritual self', 'heavenly self', 'divine self', 'angelic self', 'full-grown self', 'reborn self', and the like, repeated time and again in his writings. The new self is not born in a womb of flesh and blood, nor as a result of human desire: it is born of the Spirit (Jn 3:5). To be born of the Spirit "is to become most like God in purity, without any mixture of imperfection."[8] The conception of the new self takes place in the womb of *nada*. It grows into maturity as it gets deeply embedded in *nada*: *nada* is the only nutrition that is adequate for it, and all that is pleasing to the self obstructs the blood supply. Due to the negation of the light of reason, the womb of *nada* is quite dark. The experience of *nada* gives birth to the new self, which grows into a mature spiritual person within the realm of *nada*. Mighty things are performed by this new person, since their faculties are divine rather than human.[9] The new person is thus not only born of the Spirit, but is always moved by the same Spirit. Their will is so conformed to the will of God that they cannot opt for anything that is contrary to the will of God. Gradually they become free of all imperfections, even the habitual and involuntary movements towards evil.[10] John describes the qualitative change that takes place in the spiritual birth as a passing from the sensual to the spiritual, the animal to the rational, the "what is of man in him" to the angelic, and the human to the divine.[11]

The union of the human person with God is often described by John as a 'transforming union'; he uses various metaphors to convey how he sees this experience of love (some we have seen in chapter one).[12] In all these cases, however, the experience of *nada* is regarded as an essential prerequisite. The person must wipe their windowpane clean to allow the divine sun to penetrate the previously dark room. However, the driving force behind John's self-emptying process is love. John equates true love with the effort made towards self-purification or self-emptying:

Manifestly, then, the more the individuals through attachment and habit are clothed with their own abilities and with creatures, the less disposed they are for this union. For, they do not afford God full opportunity to transform their souls into the supernatural. As a result, individuals have nothing more to do than to strip their souls of these natural contraries and dissimilarities so that God, who is naturally communicating himself to them through nature, may do so supernaturally through grace.[13]

John introduces the metaphor of the fire and the log to further clarify the effect of God's purifying action on the individual.[14] The log, before 'acquiring' the qualities of fire and transforming itself into fire, undergoes a series of changes. It turns black and often gives off a bad odour. The person, in the process of purification, comes face to face with their ugly, miserable and sinful existence; a humiliating and painful experience. The old self with all its paraphernalia has to confront the purifying fire of *nada*. This encounter serves to reveal to the individual the nothingness of their cherished possessions and their vulnerability. Such a vision of reality is naturally a very painful experience for the ego, therefore, the individual will often try to rebel so as to save the ego from humiliation and annihilation. However, to put on the new self the old one has to be laid to rest. John gives the details of such an experience:[15]

> For the sake of further clarity in this matter, we ought to note that this purgative and loving knowledge, or divine light we are speaking of, has the same effect on a soul that fire has on a log of wood. The soul is purged and prepared for union with the divine light just as the wood is prepared for transforming into the fire. Fire, when applied to wood, first dehumidifies it, dispelling all moisture and making it give off any water it contains. Then it gradually turns the wood black, makes it dark and ugly, and even it causes it to emit a bad odour. By drying out the wood, the fire brings to light and expels all those ugly and dark accidents that are contrary to fire. Finally, by heating and enkindling it from without, the fire transforms the wood into itself and makes it as beautiful as it is itself.[16]

Among the various metaphors used by John and others
to illustrate the relationship between God and the human
person, that of the spiritual marriage receives most attention
because of its simplicity and accuracy;[17] and *nada* plays an
important role in this relationship. The lovesick bride,
who not only passionately craves for her beloved, but dares
to leave behind her home and everything to join him, is a
vivid image of a person in *nada*.[18] In other words, the
progress of the bride to her beloved is a progress on the
path of *nada*. In John's spiritual itinerary, *nada* leads to *el
todo*. The person who begins the journey with an encounter
with nada and maintains the 'courtship', becoming
accustomed to its presence will be correctly disposed for
union with God. *Nada* is an essential condition for the
spiritual marriage.

We have to bear in mind that, though frightening, the
deep plunge into the abysmal depths of *nada* is the only
means available for the person to overcome their limitations.
The person who dares to risk self-annihilation, will find
themselves in the life-giving womb of *nada*. John calls this
experience a ray of darkness.[19] It is a new consciousness
that begins to dawn within a person by means of a 'pure
and dark contemplation', which is an awareness of the
presence of God in the darkness.

Happy, beloved night of *nada*

The negative associations that, for many, often surround
John's use of the term 'night' come from a mistaken
apprehension of his intentions. John himself uses expressions
such as "glad night",[20] "glad contemplative night",[21] "O
guiding night!",[22] "O night more lovely than the dawn!",[23]
and so on, to describe the exciting "dark night that has
united the lover to the beloved".[24] It is true that in John's
writings we encounter a number of passages describing the
harsh realities of the dark night and its purifying effects.

But John always maintained that these initial sufferings are like the labour pains a woman undergoes before giving birth to her child; in this case, the birth of the happy, free new self:

> Even though this happy night darkens the spirit, it does so only to impart light concerning all things; and even though it humbles individuals and reveals their miseries, it does it only to exalt them; and even though it impoverishes and empties them of all possessions and natural affection, it does so only that they may reach out divinely to the enjoyment of all earthly and heavenly things, with a general freedom of spirit in them all.[25]

For John there are other reasons to describe the night of *nada* as 'beloved' and 'happy'.[26] At the ordinary level of consciousness, human beings are affected and controlled by the four basic human passions – joy, sorrow, hope and fear. John calls them 'winds' that disturb the equanimity of ordinary individuals by means of powerful gusts.[27] In the case of a person who lives in a state of *nada*, such battering causes little damage. Sorrow cannot affect them because of their unshakeable trust and confidence in God. According to John, such a person is even beyond compassion, which is often considered as a sure sign of sanctity.[28] The works of mercy and charity of a person residing in *nada* are flowing from nothing but goodness. A person living in the state of *nada* is beyond all passions. Like a boundless ocean they remain undisturbed and calm[29].

The practice of *nada* and the goal of *nada* are identical. As one journeys deeper and deeper into *nada* one draws closer and closer to *el todo*. *Nada* is not to be considered as an instrument to achieve a goal, but it is the goal. This does not mean that there is no cultivation of the path of *nada*, nor transformation and progress along it. It is an endless plunge into the abyss of God, which the individual considers their highest duty, yet without any certainty of success.[30]

Nada: a beginning without an end

Nada should not be understood as a goal in the sense of an end to be attained, but as the ground of the awakened life or the point of departure from which this life can begin seriously. When *nada* becomes the ground of a person's life, they approach every situation both "in the light of wisdom" and "in the light of compassion".[31] Since the person is freed from the grasping and self-interested elements in their relationships, they can live in the 'space' occupied by emptiness. Being empty of self, they are free to live for the sake of others, that is, for the sake of the creation as a whole. In this way, *nada* is the beginning of a real life, and not the end of a long road of ascetic annihilation. From the selflessness flows a compassionate love and care for the suffering parts of our own, but hitherto 'unidentified true self'. For emptiness is not a noun but a verb, its creative dynamic empties all in order to fill all. Self-emptying not only minimises the struggle for survival but also contributes towards a fuller life. The paradox is that in living this *kenosis* (of self), the person is fully alive, and in dying to their transient self, they realise their true eternal self. The death of self is thus a relative end (Jn 12:24-25). In fact, it is the beginning of the true liberated life.[32]

The realisation of *nada*, in fact, is nothing but the realisation of self because, through the *kenosis* of the ego-self, the 'original' human nature awakens in the realiser. This original nature is like that nature Tradition understands as 'existing' in Adam and Eve before their fall: an uncorrupted and newly-created state of existence. In such a state we participate in the nature of Christ, and live in Christ. To live *kenosis* means to be in the process of returning to the state of purity in which God made us. John reveals that the purifying of the person from all that is not God is the aim of his writings:

> we will present, with divine help, a way to empty and purify the
> spiritual faculties of all that is not God. By this method these

faculties can abide in the darkness of these three virtues, which
are the means and preparation, as we said, for the soul's union
with God[33]... The discreet reader must always keep in mind my
intention and goal in this book: to guide the soul in purity of
faith through all its natural and supernatural apprehensions, in
freedom from deception and every obstacle, to divine union
with God.[34]

Paradigm shift in the life of *nada*

To enter the domain of *nada*, a 'paradigm shift' is called
for. The experience of *nada* helps us wipe out the ego and
reorient ourselves to our true centre – God. According to
the paradigm by which people are generally guided, self-
realisation is the goal of life. To such a mentality the idea
of God itself is very much bound up with the idea of self-
fulfilment. The belief that the acquisition of goods will
bring about fulfilment is the motive behind almost every
human action. But in order to achieve perfect union, one
has to move from this old paradigm to the new paradigm
of total abandonment and self-surrender:

> the perfect union in this life through grace and love demands
> that they live in darkness to all the objects of sight, hearing,
> and imagination, and to everything comprehensible to the
> heart, which signifies the soul. Those are decidedly hindered,
> then, from attainment of this high state of union with God
> who are attached to any understanding, feeling, imagining,
> opinion, desire, or way of their own, or to any other of their
> works or affairs, and know not how to detach and denude
> themselves of these impediments. Their goal, as we said,
> transcends all of this, even the loftiest object that can be known
> or experienced. Consequently they must pass beyond everything
> to unknowing.[35]

The transition from one system to another always has
its uncertainties and produces its shocks, a feeling of
"hanging in mid-air"[36] as John prefers to call it. Having
been cut off from the familiar, the known and the cherished,

and not yet absorbed into the realm of the unfamiliar *nada*, one experiences fear and uncertainty.[37] The old values have been left behind and are no longer considered valid, but the new – based on pure faith, pure love and pure hope – seem unrealisable. The sense of unrelieved affliction that this state of affairs produces is due to the lack of sense-experience of God in the darkness.[38] A growth in the naked faith alone will slowly impress the awareness of the closeness of God upon the person. As the person becomes embedded in *nada*, they are able to guide their sensory and spiritual faculties in conformity with God's purpose:

> The sensory part includes body with all its senses and faculties, interior and exterior, and all natural ability (the four passions, the natural appetites, and other energies). All of this, she says, she occupies, as she does the rational and spiritual part referred to in the preceding verse, in the service of her Beloved. By directing the activity of the interior and exterior senses toward God, her use of the body is now conformed to his will. She also binds the four passions of the soul to him, for she does not rejoice except in God or hope in anything other than God; she fears only God and has no sorrow unless in relation to him. And likewise all her appetites and cares go out only to God.[39]

When the "reason and the cause of our love are grounded on God,"[40] that is, when the old paradigm of selfishness is substituted with the new paradigm of selflessness, human love is transformed into God's love and human will is transfigured into God's will. God's power sets the person free from compulsive appetites and emotional needs. We no longer use the objects of our love for our own satisfaction and the fulfilment of our unconscious drives and needs. Instead, we honour them as priceless gifts from God, to be loved with his love, for his sake, to his honour and glory, and to their blessedness. We have renounced the urge to possess the beloved emotionally and to get something for ourselves out of love and being loved.[41] Here occurs a fundamental transition from the discursive, reflective attitude of the old paradigm to a deep contemplative attitude of the new paradigm:

> Meditation is now useless for them because God is conducting them along another road, which is contemplation and is very different from the first, for the one road belongs to discursive meditation and the other is beyond the range of the imagination and discursive reflection.[42]

Nada as a *kenotic* process

John was fully convinced of the need to enter a total *kenosis* in order to arrive at *el todo*. Among the many reasons he proposes to substantiate his view, the two most radical stand out: one relating to the reality of God and a second to the reality of creatures. He writes, "God is incomprehensible and transcendent. This is why it behoves us to go to God through the negation of all."[43] From the perspective of the human subject a total emptying of possessions is essential because they often impede further progress. John writes, "Souls will be unable to reach perfection, who do not strive to be content with having nothing, in such a fashion that their natural and spiritual desire is satisfied with emptiness; for this is necessary in order to reach the highest tranquillity and peace of spirit."[44] Another argument to justify the need for this *kenosis* is the ultimate inability of human effort to achieve the desired goal: "all our works and all our trials, even though they be the greatest possible, are nothing in the sight of God. For through them we cannot give him anything or fulfil his only desire, which is the exaltation of the soul. Of these other things he desires nothing for himself, since he has no need of it."[45] That is why the lover of the 'Dark Night' poem left her home, and all she had, behind to reach her beloved; and when she reached him, she even "went out from herself" to be united with him:

I abandoned and forgot myself,
laying my face on my Beloved;
all things ceased; I went out from myself,
leaving my cares
forgotten among the lilies. [46]

But entry into the new life is not the end of the *kenotic* process. The person needs to deepen their immersion in *nada*, that is, to deepen their understanding of the truth concerning the self and God, which will lead one to further detachment from the self. As the person progresses in *kenosis*, they progress in union with God as well. In other words, the extent of our union with God is directly proportional to our progress in *kenosis*:

> in the measure that they enter into this negation and emptiness of forms through their own efforts, they will receive from God the possession of union. God effects this union in them passively, as we will explain, *Deo dante*, in the passive night of the soul. Thus God will give the habit of perfect divine union when he is pleased to do so and in accordance with the individual's preparation.[47]

The loss of all our ways of understanding the things of God, whether through the senses or 'spiritually', and the loss of personal identity are not the only, nor the major, losses that occur in the experience of *nada*. The climax of *nada* is the experience of the loss of God himself – not just feelings regarding God but the God we had come to 'work' with through theological virtues of faith, hope, and charity. This profound experience of *nada* is unavoidable if the spiritual person wishes totally to transcend all former ways of relating to God.[48] The effect of this total self-transcendence through *kenosis* is an encounter with God, so utterly 'the other', that the only way it can be experienced and expressed is as *nada*.

Nada: a passage from self-centredness to God-centredness

John holds the view that it is always the Spirit who draws us into Jesus' heart and then into the inner life of the Trinity, so that we can imitate Jesus by living the will of the Father.[49] The person becomes fully human only to the degree that they become God, by sharing in God's life.[50] This is human destiny, but it is not where the person begins: to begin they must be shattered by the awful path of *nada*, unable to rid themselves of the suspicion that they are, in fact, lost. But if they follow the example of Jesus who refused to save himself (Mk 15:30) and entrusted himself into the hands of his Father (Lk 23:47), they can repeat with the bride of the *Canticle*, "I lost myself, and was found."[51] Jesus decided to choose the will of his Father at any cost, even that of losing himself; rather than rebel, he preferred to be lost and to cast himself into the hands of his Father. This trust or commitment is the essence of his new way and new life. His obedience unto death broke the hold of the self and the world and united him once and for all with his Father. This union for which we are created can be ours if we leave behind the false self that we have created as a defence against the true self, the Christ-self.[52] In such a state we are able to experience the astounding gentleness of the inner life of God,[53] and to see the whole creation as it really is, in God, and love it with the overwhelming but gentle love with which God loves it.[54] The result of all of this is a renewed heart, made whole again. Looking at themselves from within this state of peace, the person begins to notice that many of the imperfections that used to afflict them have dropped away; they feel they are freer and more simple than they used to be. They do not get depressed or angry, and are less concerned about praise or accusation. They get more tolerant and compassionate, more free to do the work and less concerned about its fruits. The illusions of achieving

immortality through their own integrity and moral
perfection, or even the concern for progress in prayer is
given up. All these concerns are left aside as if they were
matters that are to be taken care of by God rather than
themselves, and in fact it is the creator who is more
concerned for his creatures' well-being than they are for
their own. True knowledge of the creator and his goodness
generates such a confidence in creatures that all their worries
are forgotten; full confidence in God and loyalty to his will
make the person gentle, calm and cool in the face of
difficulties.[55] God and not one's own well-being will be the
primary concern of a true lover of God:

> The soul can know clearly whether or not she loves God purely.
> If she loves him her heart or love will not be set on herself or her
> own satisfaction and gain, but on pleasing God and giving him
> honour and glory. In the measure she loves herself, that much
> less she loves God. Whether the heart has been truly stolen by
> God, will be evident in either of these two signs: if it has
> longings for God or if it finds no satisfaction in anything but
> him... Until this possession the soul is like an empty vessel
> waiting to be filled, or a hungry person craving for food, or
> someone sick and moaning for health, or like one suspended in
> the air with nothing to lean on. Such is the truly loving heart.[56]

Nada: a passage to freedom guided by the heart

The natural human person lives a life of action, desiring
and doing many things. They tie themselves to the world
by a thousand bonds, because it offers them satisfaction
and a sense of personal worth. A person's activities are
generally determined by their desires, but as a person enters
the *nada* experience, something quite new enters their life.
Previously comfortable and at home in the world, now all
that used to feel natural, normal and important seems
trivial, even laughable. The old self has died. What used to
give reason and meaning in life is shown in the light of this
dark ray to be ridiculous and even meaningless. On the

path of *nada* a person gradually rises above the natural and the supernatural faculties so as to progress from knowing into unknowing:

> Those are decidedly hindered, then, from the attainment of this high state of union with God who are attached to any understanding, feeling, imagining, opinion, desire, or way of their own, or to any other of their works or affairs, and know not how to detach and denude themselves of these impediments. Their goal, as we said, transcends all this, even the loftiest object that can be known or experienced. Consequently they must pass beyond everything to unknowing.[57]

The total self-transcendence reached through *nada* enables a person to love both God and creatures more intimately than before. In this state, their own heart becomes the person's guide as the bride in 'Dark Night' claims, "nor did I look at anything, with no other light or guide than the one that burned in my heart."[58] John was convinced that, "For the just man there is no law, he is a law unto himself."[59]

Ultimately, it is necessary to renounce even spirituality itself if we are to prepare ourselves to receive God (which after all was supposed to be the object of the exercise in the first place!).[60] John warns against all sorts of attachments:

> Thus they will be unable to reach the royal freedom of spirit attained in divine union, for freedom has nothing to do with slavery. And freedom cannot abide in a heart dominated by desires, in a slave's heart. It abides in a liberated heart, in a child's heart.[61]

Human beings have a unique potential to be aware of God's presence within them. Such awareness is a source of great power. Awareness of God's presence establishes within the individual transcendental qualities like freedom, knowledge and love, which carry them beyond their own self-imposed limits. John insists on the need for spiritual freedom. As long as we are free, we are able to know the

truth and love it because of God's presence in our free and
pure heart. John holds the view that a spiritual person on
the path of *nada* is not bound by a literal interpretation of
Scripture. Rising above the 'letter', John himself preferred
to lay bare the spiritual meanings within the Scriptural
texts. However, until a person is purified in *nada*, they are
bound by the 'outer rind' of God's revelation. John further
clarifies this point:

> In this and many other ways souls are misled by understanding
> God's locutions and revelations according to the letter, according
> to the outer rind. As has been explained, God's chief objective
> in conferring these revelations is to express and impart the spirit
> that is enclosed within the outer rind. This spirit is difficult to
> understand, much richer and more plentiful, very extraordinary
> and far beyond the boundaries of the letter. Anyone bound to
> the letter, locution, form, or figure apprehensible in the vision
> cannot avoid serious error and will later become confused for
> having been led according to the sense and not having made
> room for the spirit stripped of the letter. *Litterra, enim, occidit,
> spiritus autem vivificat* (The letter kills and the spirit gives life)
> (2 Cor. 3:6). The soul should renounce, then, the literal sense
> in these cases, and live in the darkness of faith, for faith is the
> spirit that is incomprehensible to the senses.[62]

Nada: a way of life that is natural, simple, and spontaneous

John's insistent call to emptiness might leave a casual reader
of his works with the impression that they are being asked
to empty the contents of their consciousness, like so much
rubbish from a bin, by the sheer exertion of mental muscle.
In reality John taught a kind of "effortless effort".[63] The
life of John itself is a typical example of the living of
effortless life, guided by *nada*, as one of his translators
notes: "Nothing about his life indicates that he thought he
should have a specialist's priorities in the use of his time.
He participated in all the different tasks necessary to keep a

community running."[64] John was very well aware that any effort to suppress the contents of the conscious mind would be counterproductive. Spiritual progress is flowing with the energy that God gives us to make the ascent.[65] The effects of the prayer of the quiet are chiefly peace and joy, which follow charity, and John counsels beginners not to strain themselves but be patient:

> They must be content simply with a loving and peaceful attentiveness to God, and live without the concern, without the effort, and without the desire to taste or feel him. All these desires disquiet the soul and distract it from the peaceful, quiet, and sweet idleness of the contemplation that is being communicated to it.[66]

When John invites us to 'empty our mind' he is not recommending a forced and unnatural emptying of our consciousness, but a dis-identification with the objects in it. The person meets the objects spontaneously arising in their consciousness with a non-choosing, non-reactive evenness or peace, which in turn will lead to a mental state that is virtually empty. What is being emptied is mind's natural tendency to 'stick' to objects, to react, to identify, to associate, and to wander. In the *nada* path of John, the effort involved in keeping the attention focussed and the consciousness clear is paradoxically balanced by rest, peace, a letting go, a letting be, and surrender. Here there are two mutually reciprocal wills at work – an effortful will and an effortless will, a will to attain and a will to abandon, a will to struggle and a will to submit. It is true that this way involves self-forgetfulness but at the same time it also provides the courage that enables one "to lose the herd" and walk alone. The bride in *Canticle* tells her story:

> In the inner wine cellar
> I drank of my Beloved, and, when I went abroad through all this valley,
> I no longer knew anything,
> and lost the herd that I was following.[67]

Being natural, simple, and spontaneous is the sign of fearlessness. Where there is no freedom, fear reigns. The freedom attained through *nada* is not the unmediated freedom of human will to do what it pleases, but the freedom of 'absolute nothingness' mediated in the selfless person. It is the freedom of naturalness. Human beings are made in God's image (Gen 1:26-27), but this can lead them to misunderstand what this implies and the extent to which they are similar to him (Gen 3:25). The practice of *nada* enables the person to overcome the desire to become someone other than who they really are – and to understand the truth about their kinship with God. Such a person is completely satisfied with their 'givenness' and is totally free. If or when they act, their actions do not arise from selfish motives, but are the fulfilment of God's plan. To practise this *kenotic* freedom through self-abandonment we require God's grace.

To attain the natural, simple, spontaneous and free life of *nada* is not as easy as it might appear to be. As we have mentioned earlier, for instance, many things that we do and say naturally are not 'natural' in the true sense of the word. Most of them are learned behavioural and thinking patterns. In fact, in a society with set values and programmes, spontaneity is not always appreciated. In this complicated world in which we live, any attempt to lead a natural, simple, spontaneous life, is like swimming against the tide.

Nada brings out a state of tranquillity and equanimity in the person. The heart remains steady even when everything changes.[68] In the worst sorrows and failures, the person holds fast to the supreme consolation that the will of God is always done.[69] This leads to a child-like simplicity. For a child, its parents are the reference point of its world. It may ask them a hundred questions and be fully satisfied with their answers as well as their silences! Like this child, a person in the path of *nada* is absolutely sure that what has happened, what is happening and what will happen is the best for them. They have absolute confidence in God and know that nothing can go wrong because God is with those who love him (Rom 8:28). They know that the incomprehensible God is unpredictable too, and therefore, life becomes an adventure. In fact, freedom so often comes to people when it would seem that they are most unfree, most committed, most caught up or involved. Freedom is letting God be in charge, without clinging to things and persons out of fear and desire.

The 'vanishing point' of ego-self

The encyclical letter of Pope John Paul II *Fides et Ratio* reminds us that only for those who can "look beyond themselves and their own concerns, there is the possibility of taking full and harmonious possession of their lives... (and only they can arrive at) the path of truth."[70] Selflessness in John's vision is very much related to his notion of emptiness. The essential preparation for the union with God is the emptying of soul of "all that can fall within its capacity".[71] As we have seen earlier, the term old self appears numerous times in John's writings.[72] For John the term old self means a life fully engaged and guided by the faculties of memory, intellect, will, and so on, dominated by the appetites.[73] If the hold of old self does not decrease, the power of new self cannot increase.[74] The person who fails to deny their ego makes it an idol and obeys its demands in everything. In doing so they bring misery and suffering to their fellow beings and, sooner or later, to themselves: ego-worship and suffering cannot be separated. Meanwhile, burning with the love of God, if the person resists the old self, gradually it disappears, leaving them free. Human beings are 'old' in proportion to their weakness in the theological virtues of faith, hope and charity. To be renewed fully, we must be freed from all attachments and remain in emptiness and poverty of spirit devoid of all natural as well as supernatural attachments, consolations, supports, and apprehensions. Such a state, John tells us, is the true life in union with God.[75]

There is an inescapable tendency in all those who seek to follow the spiritual path to place much faith in their good works, asceticism, practice of virtues and other devotions because such accomplishments make them appear worthy in their own eyes and give them confidence in their own capacities. They dread the thought of losing the reins of their life. When they happen to become aware of the nothingness of their ability, the futility of their efforts and of their own finitude, they experience the terrible shock of nothingness, but this frightful experience helps them to harness their desire and guides them to humility:

> Now that the soul clothed in these other garments of labour, dryness, and desolation, and its former lights have been darkened, it possesses more authentic lights in this most excellent and necessary virtue of self-knowledge. It considers itself to be nothing and finds no satisfaction in self because it is aware that of itself it neither does nor can do anything.[76]

In John's vision, the major obstacle to union with God is the person's refusal to accept their own nothingness. John exclaims, "Oh, who can explain the extent of the denial our Lord wishes of us! This negation must be similar to a temporal, natural, and spiritual death [in all things]".[77] The whole purifying action, at both the sensory and the spiritual level, has this goal: to cause the person to become disillusioned with their false self-image, which is in fact nothing but illusions produced by the seven capital sins! We have seen that these sins, when they blossom on the spiritual level are subtle and difficult to eradicate, but the urgent longings of love of God are intense enough to purge the person's impure self-love. John teaches that, "the soul is not only annihilated with respect to all things and estranged from them, but undergoes the same also with respect to herself, as if she had vanished and been dissolved in love; all of which consists in passing out of self to the Beloved."[78]

Nada: a return to the 'deepest centre,' to realise the 'home ground'

John saw the hidden presence of God in each person.[79] His presence remains unnoticed since human mind is by nature 'extrovert'. A mind with a strong tendency towards social activities will always spread out and promote itself with a view to reaching out, controlling and possessing the other. This movement of the mind goes in the opposite direction to that taken by 'centring', and leaves the person's attention dispersed among the things of the world rather than centred in their own 'home ground'. Only when they return to their 'deepest centre'[80] and empty themselves of all the preoccupations of the outside world, have they a chance to encounter the world within. This withdrawal and the resultant entry into non-discursive contemplation is an actively attentive passivity. In this state the person is possessive no more. Since God cannot fit into an occupied heart,[81] the person lets their coveted possessions go in order to make room for God. Thus the person who is fully detached and recollected waits upon the self-revealing presence of God in their innermost centre. In such a state of centring, conflicts and discords disappear. The unity rediscovered at the universal common centre of all beings, where we human beings find our true selves, brings about in the individual a total change of attitude towards the other. This centring is like a purgative fire in which the self and everything else are consumed into the oneness where ego no more exists.

By emptying themselves of every attachment the human person allows everything else in their lives to be as alive as they possible could be. Paradoxically, in the very living of this *kenosis* of the self, the person is fully alive. In dying to the self, like the grain of wheat (Jn 12:24-25), the person becomes a true life-giver. In the living realisation of *nada* the self and *nada* are dynamically identical. William Johnston puts it thus: "Life is a process of spiritualization which reaches its climax in death."[82] Death in both its material and spiritual sense. In both cases life reaches its transition point in the 'great death.' For a person who has undergone the great death of *nada*, the physical death is not a preoccupation:

> The death of such persons is very gentle and very sweet, sweeter and more gentle than was their whole spiritual life on earth. For, they die with most sublime impulses and delightful encounters of love, resembling the swan whose song is much sweeter at the moment of death.[83]

a. The deepest centre. In his *Living Flame*, John compares the mystical path to a journey into "the deepest centre of the soul",[84] where God transforms the person in love. But we can go even deeper: when we experience God within us, we find that we are in the centre along with other things, and yet, we are in an eternal movement towards the deepest centre. God is this centre that is found in all things and yet contains all things within itself:

> The deepest centre of an object we take to signify the farthest point attainable by that object's being and power and force of operation and movement... when once it arrives and no longer has any power or inclination towards further movement, we declare that it is in its deepest centre. The soul's centre is God. When it has reached God with all the capacity of its being and the strength of its operation and inclination, it will have attained its final and deepest centre in God, it will know, love, and enjoy God with all its might. When it has not reached this point (as happens in this mortal life, in which the soul cannot reach God with all its strength, even though in its centre – which is God through grace and his self-communication to it), it still has movement and strength for advancing further and is not satisfied. Although it is in its centre, it is not yet in its deepest centre, for it can go deeper in God.[85]

In his commentary on the first stanza of *Living Flame*, where John deals with the nature of the human soul, he maintains that since the soul does not have a physical, spatial existence, its deepest centre should be of the same nature. John identifies this deepest centre as the site where the ultimate purification of the person takes place. All impurities that settled in the deepest centre of the soul are burned by means of the 'living flame of love' until *nada* alone is left. For John, therefore, the deepest centre of the person in its pristine purity is *nada*. We read in his *Living Flame*:

> O living flame of love
> that tenderly wounds my soul
> in its deepest centre! Since
> now you are not oppressive,
> now consummate, if it is your will:
> tear through the veil of this sweet encounter![86]

The above two quotations from *Living Flame* show that John uses the phrase the deepest centre of soul to signify two different things. According to one account it is the point of ultimate purification.[87] From another perspective, John sees the deepest centre as God himself.[88] This ambiguity can be resolved by analysing the contexts in which these references are made. Step by step the purifying *nada* goes deeper into the person from the grosser to the subtler levels until it penetrates the innermost core of the personality and exposes every trace of egoism hidden within. As a result of this encounter with the truth, the ego is totally annihilated. Therefore, from one point of view, the deepest centre of the soul is the 'place' where *nada*, the ultimate purifier, guards against any attacks from the ego. From another point of view, this abode of *nada* is the 'Empty Ark of the Covenant' where God chooses to reside.[89] When there is nothing between God and the person there is no more separation. When God becomes the centre of our being, we find ourselves through the Trinity in a fullness of love that embraces all creation. At the depth of our being, we transcend our limited selves in Being through the vanishing point of the ego and find our unity with all beings through the Trinity:

It should be known that the Word, the Son of God, together
with the Father and the Holy Spirit, is hidden by his essence
and his presence in the innermost being of the soul. Individuals
who want to find him should leave all things through affection
and will, enter within themselves in deepest recollection, and
let all things be as though not.[90]

b. The home ground of creation. There are two ways in
which human beings are united to God. The first is a
natural or essential union which is part of our very nature
as human beings and exists without any regard to merit.
The second type of union is supernatural and is acquired
through personal co-operation with God and a transformation.[91] For John this supernatural union is in fact the
conscious realisation of the natural union. In other words,
it is a conscious actualisation of what is given naturally. It
adds nothing to the natural union. The consciousness of
our being naturally united to God reminds us that we are
not the centres of the universe, nor even the true centre of
our own selves! Using the then controversial Copernican
theory,[92] John explains: we are attached to God as the
material things are attached to the earth. When the earth
moves, all the material things in it move.[93] God is the
home ground; he, in fact, is the single centre of all beings
including ourselves. Using the vision of Isaiah (Is 9:6) John
compares God to the great ruler who governs all creation;[94]
and all beings, in heaven and on the earth and under it, are
upheld by God (Phil 2:10). The power of the Word of
God (Heb 1:3) moves all things in unison. This 'ground'[95]
of everything is God, discovered as 'being' itself at the
depth of all beings. This ground that we find within us is
not something that we contain, rather, it contains us. It is
something in which we participate along with everything
else in creation. Supernatural union, then, is a conscious
realisation of and lived participation in the union, which,
though present by the nature of existence itself, is something
we are not ordinarily conscious of:

To understand the nature of this union, one should first know
that God sustains every soul and dwells in it substantially, even
though it may be that of the greatest sinner in the world. This
union between God and creatures always exists. By it he
conserves their being so that if the union should end they
would immediately be annihilated and cease to exist.
Consequently, in discussing union with God we are not
discussing the substantial union that always exists, but the
soul's union with and transformation in God that does not
always exists, except when there is likeness of love. We will call
it the union of likeness; and the former, the essential or
substantial union. The union of likeness is supernatural; the
other natural. The supernatural union exists when God's will
and the soul's are in conformity, so that nothing in the one is
repugnant to the other. When the soul rids itself completely of
what is repugnant and unconformed to the divine will, it rests
transformed in God through love.[96]

John's mysticism is dominated by the notion of returning
to the source. By returning to *nada,* that is, to *el todo,*
creatures can rediscover their lost fellowship and their
common home ground. A total negation of the ego-self,
through a gradual *kenosis* of our self-centredness, dispels
the distrust habitually we extend to other creatures, and
the original nature awakens in us, accomplishing a re-entry
into the lost paradise! The person who gets this far will
have neither a domineering attitude nor a pragmatic desire
to manipulate their fellow beings for their own ends. Such
a person understands all creatures and lives in full harmony
with them. Their vision and philosophy will never again be
ego-centred or even person-centred. They will not only
respond compassionately to the miseries and sufferings of
human beings, but also resist the abuse and exploitation of
animate and inanimate beings, as they realise that everything
together forms 'one bride':

> And though beings and places
> were divided in this way,
> yet all form one,
> who is called the bride;

for love for the same Bridegroom
made one bride of them. [97]

Nada: a life of constant awareness of God's presence

Although God is hidden from us both in his transcendence
and immanence, this does not mean that he is remote from
his creation: he is hidden in its deepest centre and is
present as its home ground. Those who withdraw their
eyes from the outer world to the inner world cannot miss
the presence of the Triune God.[98] But this turning to God
in recollection can only be done through the practice of the
theological virtues. Even in the persecution that fell on
him, John saw the hand of God and urged others not to
speak uncharitably of his persecutors, but to think "only
that God ordains all."[99] He wrote that trust in God should
be so great that even if the whole world were to collapse
one should not become disturbed.[100] He felt certain that
the enduring of situations with equanimity reaps many
blessings, and helps a person in the middle of adversity to
make clear judgements and choose the right option. This
total trust gave John peace and serenity on his deathbed.
When reminded of all that he had suffered, he replied with
these remarkable words, "Padre, this is not the time to be
thinking of that; it is by the merits of the blood of our Lord
Jesus Christ that I hope to be saved."[101] John was fully
aware that since love brings an equality between the lover
and the beloved, the person immersed in loving attentiveness
towards God experiences God's own life and enjoys divine
bliss and blessedness,[102] without getting tainted by the
impurity that a life of attachment brings with it. In the
state of nada, both God and the human person experience
the same love and the same delight. John proclaims that
God delights in all things since the creative beauty that
God originally placed in all creatures remains unaffected,

whatever their current relationship to him might be.[103] As a result of the experience of *nada*, a person is enabled to notice in everything the indwelling of God and takes delight in all things, without clinging to anything.[104] John concludes that, "just as God is incapable of feeling any distaste, neither does the person feel any, for the delight of God's glory is experienced and enjoyed in the substance of the soul now transformed in him."[105] He recommends this very same attitude of equanimity or the passive attitude of *nada* even when God directly reveals himself. In fact, normally, one experiences nothing in these moments because there is nothing that one ought or is able to do in this regard. It is a waiting for God [106] with ever increasing awareness, attentiveness, and love. It implies a wakefulness and alertness while remaining in profound stillness within:[107]

> God it is who is working now in the soul, and for this reason the soul can do nothing. Consequently, these persons can neither pray vocally nor be attentive to spiritual matters, nor still attend to temporal affairs and business.[108]... They should allow the soul to remain in rest and quietude even though it may seem obvious to them that they are doing nothing and wasting time, and even they think this disinclination to think about anything is due to their laxity. Through patience and perseverance in prayer, they will be doing a great deal without activity on their part.[109]

Nada: constant 'yes' and boundless openness

Nada, in a way, is simply a resting in God, a method of abandoning ourselves to God. Through practice, we develop an ability to abandon ourselves to this state in trust that is God's will for us and even of willing it because God wills it. As Barbara Dent puts it, "I just have to wait, that is my work. Waiting. Waiting is my work. My work is waiting. Lord, help me to wait well. Help me to wait patiently and in peace."[110] *Nada* is the boundless openness which waits without demands and conditions. To centre ourselves in God is to change the whole orientation of our being. Such an attitude means we must silence our desire for this or that. But more than just saying 'no' to certain things, this silence is the result of saying 'yes' to God and living in the awareness of that 'yes' which has been pronounced. John describes the bride as an open door waiting for the beloved: "The bride must first be a door in order to receive the re-enforcement of cedar wood; that is, she must hold the door of her will open to the Bridegroom so he may enter through the complete and true 'yes' of love."[111]

The proper response to the invitation to *nada* lies not in the addition of further activities, but rather in their subtraction: an undoing of mental activity so that God's activity may proceed unimpeded in the human psyche. For John, one of the beneficial effects of the experience of nothingness is that it grounds the person in the virtue of humility. According to him, the action of God in the life of an individual is not time-bound or intermittently dispensed. It is available to the person always and everywhere. Once the person empties themselves by entering the *nada* consciousness, they have already opened themselves to the action of grace. John says:

> In this solitude away from all things, the soul is alone with God and he guides, moves and raises her to divine things... Once the soul disencumbers these faculties and empties them of everything inferior and of possessiveness in regard to superior things, leaving them alone without these things, God engages them in the invisible and the divine. It is God who guides her in this solitude.[112]

Desire for or attachment to anything other than God is the result of self-love. God must be sought for his own sake. The person must not allow the innumerable blessings, consolations and benefits they come across to distract them from the beloved. On these grounds John considers it seriously wrong to have more regard for God's blessings than for God himself.[113] As we have already mentioned, an emptying of the self of all those things within the individual's power to let go is the essential preparation for union with God.[114] Here we can notice an echo of the great monastic ideal of *vacare Deo,* being free for God. The person considers themselves as nothing and has no satisfaction in themselves; for they see that of themselves they can do nothing.[115] John advises, "Keep habitual confidence in God, esteeming in yourself and in your sisters those things that God most values, which are spiritual goods."[116] Those who fall asleep (Lk 12:37) or come too late (Mt 25:10) or have other things to do (Mt 22:5) fail to be available to the bridegroom. Even Jesus' friend Martha may have compromised her availability, but her sister Mary opted for the 'better way', renunciation (Lk 10:42) through which she made herself totally available to her beloved. John beautifully expresses the longings of love and the attitude of boundless openness in the following prayer:

> Lord God, my Beloved, if you still remember my sins in such a way that you do not do what I beg of you, do your will concerning them my God, which is what I most desire, and exercise your goodness and mercy, and you will be known through them. And if you are waiting for my works so as to hear my prayer through their means, grant them to me, and work them for me, and the sufferings you desire to accept, and let it be done. But if you are not waiting for my works, what is it that makes you wait, my most clement Lord? Why do you delay?[117]

Nada: total availability to God's action

Taking no initiative or doing nothing is not what is meant by abandonment to the will of God. The view that abandonment is the absence of enthusiasm and personal effort makes a mockery of all our God-given talents and potential. The practice of abandonment has two aims: the restraining of the over-zealous tendencies of the ego, and the prevention of a total collapse of self-determination at the face of disheartening setbacks. Abandonment is not inertness. Human beings can reach perfection only by exercising their capacity as intelligent, conscious beings; all their faculties should be perfected through their proper use. Because God never dictates moment to moment what he requires of us, we must learn to use all our bodily and spiritual faculties to discern the will of God in various situations. In the third book of *Ascent*, John seems to convey that there is a loss of the use of memory and imagination at the summit of the mystical states, but his own life and treatises provide us ample proof of the fact that he was in full possession of these faculties. This means that the suppression of the memory and the imagination applies, not to everyday actions, but to times of sublime contemplation and specially graced moments.[118]

Extreme self-awareness and the anxious desire that God remove all faults and imperfections immediately are motivated by a desire for inner peace rather than love of God.[119] As we have noted earlier, John puts forward Jesus, who died on the cross, was plunged into suffering, brought to nothing, forsaken by the Father, as the model of abandonment. His advice was to follow the model of Christ and to embrace the total divesting of self, poverty and total detachment from all things for Christ's sake. Unless we practise self-abandonment, we cannot know Christ. John assures us that a person who is living in aridity and trial, but who submits to the dictates of reason, is more pleasing to God than one that does everything with consolation, yet fails in this submission:[120]

> It is always vain to be disturbed, since being disturbed is never of any help. Thus if the whole world were to crumble and come to an end and all things were to go wrong, it would be useless to get disturbed, for this would do more harm than good. Enduring all with tranquil and peaceful equanimity not only reaps many blessings but also helps the soul so that in these very adversities it may manage better in judging them and employing the proper remedy.[121]

In the same way, it was not the personal efforts of the bride that helped her to "catch the foxes",[122] "to still the north wind"[123] and "to calm the girls of Judea",[124] all of which were obstacles to the full delight of the state of spiritual union, but the ardent longings of the bridegroom. Once all the things that distracted her have been stilled, the bride finds delightful rest in the arms of her beloved and becomes God through participation, as far as possible in this life. We have already seen how John bases his argument on biblical revelation to substantiate this view. He argues, "Just as in the consummation of the carnal marriage where there are two in one flesh, as Sacred Scripture points out (Gen 2: 24), so also when the spiritual marriage between God and the soul is consummated, there are two natures in one spirit and love."[125] Once the destination, 'the sweet garden of her desire', is reached, there is no further need for the soul to strive for progress in an active way. Further progress is brought about by her total surrender and passivity to the will of her beloved. It is a restful stage of inexplicable delight and spiritual ecstasy.

As we have noted before, the great desire and longing for union not only preoccupies the person but also God himself. The purpose of creation was this union and love-relationship. Once the union and the love-relationship were interrupted by sin, the Creator more even than creation sought to restore this broken relationship. Aware of her own wretchedness, the bride hid herself from the bridegroom, and it was the bridegroom who went out in search of his bride, paid himself the full price of her failure and washed her clean in his blood and led her to his bridal chamber:

> Great was the desire of the bridegroom to free and ransom his bride completely from the hands of sensuality and the devil. Like the good shepherd rejoicing and holding on his shoulders the lost sheep for which he has searched along many winding paths (Lk 15:4-5)... this loving Shepherd and Bridegroom rejoices. And it is wonderful to see his pleasure in carrying the

rescued, perfected soul on his shoulders, held there by his hands in this desired union.[126]

Nada: sacrament par excellence

A sacrament is a sacred sign by which we worship God, he reveals his love to us and accomplishes his saving work in us.[127] It has been argued that in John's mystical theology nada becomes a uniquely efficacious 'sacrament' of God's presence.[128] The experience of nada becomes a means through which God is present, in a way that no scripture, no sacrament, no doctrine nor any person was able to be. Nada, for John, transmits God more effectively than anything created because "nothingness does not resist"[129] the advent of God. Nada represents God in a far more comprehensive and appropriate way than all other signs and symbols we use. Its unlimitedness and incomprehensibility make it the best sign to represent God. Entry into nada is the best means to become a partaker in God's nature. In other words, a person who experiences nada, is God by participation.[130] The spiritual person's inability to pray and meditate while undergoing the experience of nada actually liberates them to enter divine contemplation, and nada awaits the seeker at the end of the nada path: as we have noted earlier, the ultimate destination is the "place where no one appears".[131]

Nada: the perfect sign of the invisible

In the second chapter of the first book of Ascent John provides three reasons for calling the journey towards union with God a 'night'.[132] The third reason, which is the most fundamental according to him, is that, "God is a dark night to the soul in this life". Any god found outside the 'dark cloud' is a false god. King Solomon exclaimed, "The

Lord has said that he would live in the thick darkness" (1 Kgs 8:12). Therefore, only those who remain in *nada* alone are entitled to receive the "secret and intimate" communication with God.[133] For this reason John calls *nada* "the happy hiding place of heart".[134] *Nada* always remains a place where 'no one appears', and precisely because of this it becomes the place where the spiritual person encounters and is united to God. We cannot imagine a more perfect sign other than *nada* to represent God. In fact, *nada* even surpasses the limitations of signs and symbols. *Nada* not only indicates, but it is the ground where God is present in his fullness.

For John, to enter *nada* is to transcend all limitations. In other words, the experience of transcendence is an experience of *nada*. That is the reason why at each advancing step on the path of the perfect spirit John inscribed *nada*, *nada*. Spiritual evolution is a progression from *nada* to *nada* till one reaches the summit of the mount; however, as we mentioned earlier, John does not define *nada* solely as a means for climbing the mount, a means toward the union, its role is even more fundamental: even on the mount *nada*. The ascending process of negation is accomplished by the denial of all human desires, both material and spiritual. This journey to *nada* is a journey to the truth and reality of ourselves, and of God. John's God is totally transcendent, dwelling above conventional human language, concepts, imaginings, and ideals. It is a God who does not yield to any human representation, but makes his abode in *nada*. Therefore, *nada* is the perfect sign that represents God in his fullness. Through *nada* John let God remain as he is and refused to dishonour him by personifying him according to his human imagination. In doing so he was obeying God's stern directive to the Israelites not to represent him, neither with the material nor with the spiritual:

In neither looking nor being able to look at anything, the soul
is not detained in her journey to God by anything outside him,
for in her advance she is free of hindrance from the forms and
figures of the natural apprehensions, which are those that usually
prevent her from being always united with the being of God.[135]

Nada: channel of God's grace

In the fourth chapter of the first book of *Ascent* John
repeats the word *nada* more than twelve times in order to
highlight the absolute nature of the negation that is needed
to arrive at *el todo*.[136] But he never proposed that human
effort is able to bring us to *el todo*. By remaining immersed
in *nada*, we are expressing our longings for God. *Nada* is
the channel down which God's grace and energy flow.
Entry into *nada* is painful: "In the substance of the soul
they [who are being purified] suffer abandonment, supreme
poverty, dryness, cold, and sometimes heat. They find
relief in nothing, nor does any thought console them, nor
can they even raise the heart to God, so oppressed are they
by this flame."[137] But though the painful process of
purification brings suffering on the person, it also heals
them, and as they become immersed in *nada*, the experience
generates in the person a stability of mind that is not
shaken by gain or loss, respect or disrespect, praise or
blame, happiness or suffering. This does not mean that a
person in *nada* is beyond all feelings and emotions. They
continue to experience positive and negative feelings and
sensations, but are not carried away by them. In other
words, the heart does not become defiled by hate, greed,
confusion, attachment or clinging, which can pollute the
clear water of interiority and disturb the pool of
contemplation and the flowers that float upon it, namely
care, kindness, and other virtues of the transformed life. In
fact, such a person practises some of John's most
fundamental principles:

To reach satisfaction in all,
desire satisfaction in nothing.
To come to the knowledge of all,
desire the knowledge of nothing.
To come to possess all,
desire the possession of nothing.
To arrive at being all
desire to be nothing.[138]

In these verses, *nada* is juxtaposed four times with *todo*. John teaches that we reach union with *el todo* by negating the desire for everything else, and expresses this idea forcefully in the couplet, "to come to be what you are not/ you must go by a way in which you are not." The lines which conclude the above verses speak of the freedom given by this experience of *nada*, "In this nakedness the spirit finds its quietude and rest, for in coveting nothing, nothing tires it by pulling it up, and nothing oppresses it by pushing it down, because it is at the centre of its humility."[139] John reassures us that the person who is in *nada* is beyond the reach of the "watching fears of night"[140].

> Finally the "watching fears of night" do not reach her, for she is now so clearly illuminated and strong and rests so firmly in her God that the devils can neither cause her obscurity through their darkness nor frighten her with their terrors, nor awaken her by their attacks. Nothing can reach or molest her now that she has withdrawn from all things and entered into her God where she enjoys all peace, tastes all sweetness, and delights in all delights insofar as this earthly state allows.[141]

John further adds, "There is another exceptional and principal benefit of detachment from joy in creatures: freedom of heart for God. With this, the soul is disposed for all the favours God will grant it. Without it he does not bestow them."[142] Thus for John, *nada* is the channel of all the graces God gives us. Moreover, as mentioned earlier this total detachment elevates a person to be like God, in action and attitude: "By not becoming attached to anyone, despite these apparent and deceptive natural goods, a person remains unencumbered and free to love all, rationally and spiritually, which is the way God wants them to be loved."[143] Human love now finds its true depth and a new freedom – loving our fellows rationally and spiritually as God wants them loved. If such love involves attachment, then we must be certain that we are more attached to God:

> By liberating themselves from joy in temporal goods, they not only free themselves from the pestiferous kinds of harm... but in addition acquire the virtue of liberality. Liberality is one of God's principal attributes and can in no way coexist with covetousness. Moreover, they acquire liberty of spirit, clarity of reason, rest, tranquillity, peaceful confidence in God, and, in their will, the true cult and homage of God. They obtain more joy and recreation in creatures through the dispossession of them. They cannot rejoice in them if they behold them with possessiveness, for this is a care that, like a trap, holds the spirit to earth and does not allow wideness of heart (2 Cor. 6:11). In the detachment from things they acquire a clearer knowledge of them and a better understanding of both natural and supernatural truths concerning them. Their joy, consequently, in these temporal goods is far different from the joy of one who is attached to them, and they receive great benefits and advantages from their joy. The delight they have in these goods derives from what is good and true in them, as they were intended to be enjoyed.[144]

Jesus and Mary: perfect models of '*nada*-life'

John was fully convinced of the truth of Jesus' solemn declaration, "I am the way" (Jn 14:6). And John knew that the way of Jesus was that of absolute *kenosis*. In Mary, he perceived the perfect follower of that way. Progress on the path of *nada* depends on the person's ability to follow Jesus and Mary in their path. The *kenotic* process of Jesus began in the manger in Bethlehem and continued through his baptism (Mk 1:9-11) until his second baptism on the cross in which he bowed before the will of God (Mk 10:35; Lk 12:50). Jesus died to his senses, spiritually throughout his life and naturally at his death. For, as he said of himself, he had nowhere in life to lay his head (Mt 8:20). In death he had even less! The Gospels of Mark and Matthew depict his abandonment, both interior and exterior (since neither his disciples nor his Father left him without any consolation and relief): "My God, my God, why have you forsaken me?" (Mt 27:46; Mk 15:34). Mary too, from the moment she said 'yes' to the angel Gabriel, until she received her son's battered body from the cross, walked the way of *nada*. These examples help us to understand the mystery of *nada* as the door as well as the way to union with God. We accomplish a greater work, the more we annihilate ourselves in matters of senses as well as of spirit for the sake of God. When we are reduced to nothing in the most profound form of humiliation, union with God is effected, which is the highest stage a person can reach while on this earth. John places before us the lives of Jesus and Mary as the best illustrations of the fact that spiritual advancement does not consist in spiritual refreshment, delights and feelings, but in a living death on the cross – dead to the worlds of both the senses and the spirit.[145]

"Your will be done" (Mt 26:39): the perfect expression of *nada*

The essence of the life of Jesus was to do the will of his Father.[146] Total submission to the will of his Father was the secret of his ultimate success. Therefore, Jesus is the perfect model of the *kenotic* path. Out of his obedience and love towards his Father he became *nada*. Obedient, Jesus knew many failures. Right from the outset, John directs our attention to Christ, the model upon whom each person must pattern their life:

First, have habitual desire to imitate Christ in all your deeds by bringing your life into conformity with his. You must then study his life in order to know how to imitate him and behave in all events as he would. Second, in order to be successful in this imitation, renounce and remain empty of any sensory satisfaction that is not purely for the honour and glory of God. Do this out of love for Jesus Christ. In his life he had no other gratification, nor desired any other, than the fulfilment of his Father's will, which he called his meat and food (Jn 4:34)[147]

John was profoundly focused upon Christ. Jesus Christ was his model on the path to union. For John, Jesus is the eternal mediator in our union with God. Jesus was a man who never exercised his talents for his own advantage, but regarded everything he had as a gift received from his Father (Jn 16:28). He was fully committed to the will of the Father and his Kingdom. It was this uncompromising dedication to his Father's mission that brought him untold sufferings, and in the end crucifixion. At the crucial moment of his greatest trial his Father hid his face. But Jesus did not rebel. The abandonment until death practised by Jesus ultimately proved not to be an illusion. The seeds of rebellion are incapable of germinating in a soil that has been prepared, following Christ's example: with the determination to take a path of humility, to submit to God, and even to die.[148]

As we have mentioned, the life of Jesus was a continuous *kenosis*.[149] On the cross Jesus became the perfect example of emptiness and spiritual poverty – the 'poor man of God'. Jesus was so free that he was never burdened by his self-interests or the selfish interests of others. He chose to serve rather than to be served. He did not worry about what the world would think of him or do with him. The cry of Christ while experiencing the abandonment of his Father[150] was soon followed by an absolute surrender of himself into the hands of the invisible and incomprehensible God. Every person in his path towards God must enter the midnight darkness of faith, which is the secure way to God. In fact, contemplation is nothing but an experience of this ray of darkness piercing the heart. John refused to consider any spirituality worthwhile that abandons this path of *nada*:

> Accordingly, I would not consider any spirituality worthwhile that wants to walk in sweetness and ease and run from the imitation of Christ. Because I have said that Christ is the way and that this way is a death to our natural selves in the sensory and spiritual parts of the soul, I would like to demonstrate how this death is patterned on Christ's, for he is our model and light.[151]

Mary's *fiat*: the typical response of the *nada*-life

Hans Urs von Balthasar wrote, "If the Son's life is described as an ever-deepening *kenosis*, the Mother's is its faithful accompaniment."[152] John's doctrine of *nada* aimed at purifying the person of all their attachments, which John saw Mary[153] as having fully achieved in her life.[154] The life of Mary reveals the practice of a constant and intimate union with God: she demonstrates how to be responsive to the work of the Holy Spirit; she was moved always by the Spirit; the Spirit did not descend on Mary merely at the moment of Incarnation, but was already active in her. John presents Mary as the model of a person who lives in harmony with the will of God:[155] she shows the way to prayer; she teaches how to suffer, and how to care for the afflicted; she was always guided by the Spirit in her decisions, and consequently, she undertook only 'appropriate' work. In short, her actions were the actions of God:

> Such was the prayer and work of our Lady, the most glorious Virgin. Raised from the beginning to this high state, she never had the form of any creature impressed in her soul, nor was she moved by any, for she was always moved by the Holy Spirit.[156]

Mary was so thoroughly fashioned by God's Spirit and attached to his will that through his 'overshadowing' she

was able to give birth to the God-man.[157] Mary committed
every fibre of her being to the implementation of God's
loving will for his creation. Her ability to bring forth new
life was permeated by her response to God so that she
became the mother of God. Mary was so ego-free that she
collaborated with the eternal plan of God, and in Luke's
Gospel rejoices that God has seen her emptiness and looked
with favour at his "handmaiden" (Lk 1:48). The redemptive
kenosis of Jesus began in the womb of Mary when she
emptied her will by giving *fiat* to God's will. As the *kenosis*
of God in Christ grew in her womb, her own progress in
self-*kenosis* is reflected in her concern for others, going to
help Elizabeth (Lk 1:36-40). Mary was a continuous 'yes'
to the call of both God and his creation. When Jesus was
twelve years old, Mary lost him in the temple; finding him
she asked him why he had abandoned her, and he answered
her with another why (Lk 2:48-50). This 'why' of Mary
prefigures the 'why' of her Son on the cross (Mk 15:34).
But the unspoken answers to both the 'whys' are the same
– the Father's will. At the marriage feast at Cana we find
that Mary's selfless compassion turns her into an instrument
in her Son's ministry (Jn 2:1-11). Her ministry of selfless
co-operation ultimately culminates in the crucifixion. When
Jesus assigned John to her as her Son, in the place of her
eternal Son she silently accepted a mortal son (Jn 19:26-
27). Thus her *kenosis* reached its climax.

Mary is the perfect model of prayer. Even when she
brought an urgent problem to her Son, she knew the final
decision rested with him. We hear her telling the servants,
"Do whatever he tells you to do" (Jn 2:5). Perhaps we hear
an echo of her *fiat* in these words. This is a clear proof of
her trust in the goodness and wisdom of her Son. Mary was
'actively passive' and 'passively active' throughout her life.
She has contributed to humanity, through her passivity,
more than any of those so-called 'active' lovers of humanity.
She was never stubborn in her demands.[158] Even as the
Mother of God she remained a handmaid and never called

herself the 'bride'.[159] Her heart goes out to the needy, not with a sense of patronage or self-promotion, but with that of real sympathy and charity.[160]

John furthermore presents Mary as the model for those who suffer.[161] According to John, the reasons for human suffering are many, but any response should be like that of Mary. Mary could not have perhaps understood fully why her beloved son who had not done any wrong should suffer and die like a criminal, but her strong faith and unrelenting hope in God helped her to undergo all the suffering with the same attitude of *fiat*.[162] The state of perfection to which Mary was raised was not static. Having been permitted to suffer, Mary could and did develop in perfection and love, and her spiritual life grew in intensity. Even though the angel Gabriel greeted her "full of grace" (Lk 1:28), her *fiat*, her total and unreserved 'yes', could not but merit an increase of grace within her, especially as a result of her surrender which made itself manifest in a way of sorrow from the moment of Christ's conception to his death on Calvary.[163]

Conclusion

John not only brought the concept of *nada* to its fullest and richest expression but, more significantly, contributed a unique mystical theology to Christianity. To this day, his achievement has not been surpassed. The concept of *nada* presented in his mystical theology bears all the signs of a knowledge gained through experience rather than an aura of philosophical reflection. Perhaps it was his deep and direct encounter with *nada* that revealed to him *el todo* and enabled him to approach it. According to him, *nada* is the ground on which *el todo* can be established. He also understood that *nada* was not only the 'cause' but also the 'effect' of the union or encounter with *el todo*. The frequent use of the word *nada* and its synonyms like nakedness, poverty of spirit, 'as though non-existent', void, privation, purgation, negation, resignation, annihilation, emptiness, and so on, which occur in an almost antiphonal way in his writings are convincing proof that the experience of *nada* is both central and absolute to his mystical theology.

Those who have undergone the *nada* experience become integrated persons sharply focussed on God. There is no more resistance to suffering, or craving for pleasure. God becomes their centre and nothing is likely to draw them out of their orbit. A life of *nada* is not simply a remaining inert before the inscrutable decrees of the Absolute. Rather, it is the living of *kenosis* guided by the spirit of Jesus. In that true life of self-forgetfulness the person is conscious of God's Spirit that is at work within. This Sprit becomes the basis of their true life so that they can act spontaneously with the clear mind and generous heart of Jesus. *Nada* cannot be lived through an exercise of the human will since that very wilful effort must itself be emptied out. In other words, we do not live *nada*, rather, it is *nada* that makes us live. The self or ego, therefore, must completely disappear, and this is the focal point of John's teaching. This is precisely the experience of *nada* in the vision of John. It is a freedom from the ego-self that is accomplished by the *kenosis* of emptiness itself. A person must be conscious of their self no longer; they must be selfless. We cannot form ourselves this way; we must be formed this way by the free action of God who both abides in *nada* and reveals himself in it.

The 'grain' of ego that falls into the 'womb' of *nada* is not merely transformed or changed. The old self suffers a real death and there emerges a new self which has nothing in common with the old self. Thanks to the absence of the ego this new creature is totally available to God. In living by the new paradigm of *kenosis* this new creature, who has renounced the role of aggressor, may be called upon to take on themselves that of victim. Remaining in *nada*, the new creature becomes a living sacrament and a channel of grace.

Since they live in the deepest centre and know their home ground, they are in full harmony with the rest of the creation which together makes one bride. In Mary we have the human prototype of the mystical bride; in Jesus we have the archetype of the divine bridegroom. The essence of the many aspects of *nada* is described by John himself in a letter written by him to Doña Juana de Pedraza on 12 October 1589:

> Since you walk in these darkness and voids of spiritual poverty, you think that everyone and everything is failing you. It is no wonder that in this it also seems that God is failing you. But nothing is failing you, neither do you have to discuss anything, nor is there anything to discuss, nor do you know this, nor will you find it, because all of these are doubts without basis. Those who desire nothing else than God walk not in darkness, however poor and dark they are in their own sight. And those who walk not presumptuously, or according to their own satisfactions, whether from God or from creatures, nor do their own will in anything, have nothing to stumble over or discuss with anyone. You are making good progress. Do not worry, but be glad![164]

NOTES

1 *LF* 4,6.
2 *1A* 6,4.
3 W. Johnston, *The Mystical Way,* 69.
4 *LF* 4,6.
5 *2N* 9,5.
6 *LF* 4,5.
7 J. Dupuis, *Jesus Christ at the Encounter of World Religions,* Faith meets Faith Series (Maryknoll, N.Y.: Orbis Books, 1993), 70.
8 *2A* 5,5; *2N* 9,6.
9 *2A* 3,3.
10 *LF* 2,33.
11 *3A* 26,3.
12 *2A* 5,6.
13 *2A* 5,4.
14 *2N* 10,1-5.
15 *1A* 5,7; *2A* 5,5.
16 *2N* 10,1.

17 *C* 22,3.
18 *C* 1,22; 2,5-6; 3,10.
19 *2N* 5,3; *C* 14-15,16.
20 N. Stanza, 3.
21 *2N* 25,2.
22 'Dark Night', stanza 5. *The Collected Works of St John of the Cross* (tr., K. Kavanaugh and O. Rodriguez), 711.
23 *Ibid.*
24 *Ibid.*
25 *2N* 9,1.
26 *Letter* 16. *The Collected Works of St John of the Cross* (tr., K. Kavanaugh and O. Rodriguez), 697.
27 *1A* 6,6.
28 *C* 20-21,10.
29 *C* 20-21,10-11.
30 E. Underhill, *Mysticism*, 92.
31 *Ibid.* 50.
32 Cf. E. Underhill, *Mysticism*, 171.
33 *2A* 6,6.
34 *2A* 28,1.
35 *2A* 4,4.
36 *2N* 6,5.
37 *2N* 9,7.
38 *2N* 6,5.
39 *C* 28,4.
40 *3A* ,23,1.
41 B. Dent, *My Only Friend* , 94.
42 *1N* 10,2.
43 *2A* 24,9.
44 *Sayings* 54.
45 *C* 28,1.
46 'Dark Night', stanza 8.
47 *3A* ,2,13.
48 *2N* 5-7.
49 *1A* 13,3-4.
50 *LF* 2,34.
51 *C* 29,10.
52 T. Kane, *Gentleness in John of the Cross* (Oxford: SLG Press, 1985), 3.
53 *LF* 2,16-19.
54 *LF* 4,5.
55 Cf. T. Kane, *Gentleness*, 18.
56 *C* 9,5-6. See also *C* 1,14 and *LF* 1,32.
57 *2A* 4,4.
58 'Dark Night', stanza 3. *The Collected Works of St John of the Cross* (tr., K. Kavanaugh and O. Rodriguez), 711.
59 Written at the top of the 'Sketch of Mount Carmel', cf. *The Collected Works of St John of the Cross* (tr., K. Kavanaugh and O. Rodriguez), 111.

60 P. Spearritt, "Empty in pure negation: Theological and practical implications of taking God seriously", in P. Slattery (ed.), *St John of the Cross* (New York: St Paul's, 1994),144.

61 *1A* 4,6; *1A* 15,2.

62 *2A* 19,5.

63 *1N* 10,4.

64 *The Collected Works of St John of the Cross* (tr., K. Kavanaugh and O. Rodriguez), 26.

65 S. Muto, *John of the Cross for today: The Dark Night* (Notre Dame: Ave Maria Press, 1994), 296.

66 *1N* 10,4.

67 *C* Stanza, 17.

68 S. Muto, *Steps Along the Way*, 71.

69 *LF* 1,32.

70 P. John Paul II, *Fides et Ratio*, n.15.

71 *2A* 4,2.

72 *1A* 5,7; *2A* 5,5; *2N* 2,1; 3,3; 4,2; 6,1; 9,4; 16,4; *C* 20-21,1; *LF* 2,3; Caut. 2.

73 *1A* 5,7.

74 *LF* 2,23.

75 *2N* 9,4.

76 *1N* 12,2.

77 *2A* 7,6.

78 *C* 26,14.

79 *C* 1,6.

80 *LF* 1,11-13.

81 *LF* 3,48.

82 W. Johnston, *The Mystical Way*, 81.

83 *LF* 1,30.

84 *LF* 1,9-14.

85 *LF* 1,11-12.

86 *LF* Stanza 1.

87 'Living Flame' 1,8.

88 See also *LF* 1,9-10 and *LF* 1,8.

89 *1A* 5,7.

90 *C* 1,6.

91 *2A* 5,3.

92 This was a very daring act on the part of John, since the Copernican theory was not accepted at that time. That is why in the first edition of his work (1618), the editor changed the text to read "if the earth were to move, all natural things in it would move." This change was made because by the time the first edition appeared, Copernicus' work was on the Index of forbidden books.

93 *LF* 4,4.

94 *LF* 4,4.

95 *LF* 1,11.

96 *2A* 5,3.

97 P. Romances, *On creation*, lines, 120-125.

  98 *C* 1,6.
  99 *Letter* 26.
 100 *Counsels to a Religious on How to Reach Perfection*, 2, cf. *The Collected Works of St John of the Cross* (tr., K. Kavanaugh and O. Rodriguez), 725-726.
 101 *Ibid.* 28.
 102 *C* 31,1; 31,28.
 103 *C* 20-21,12.
 104 *C* 20-21,12.
 105 *C* 22,5.
 106 B. Dent, *My Only Friend*, 32-33.
 107 S. Muto, *The Journey Homeward* (New Jersey: Dimension Books, 1977), 65.
 108 *2N* 8,1.
 109 *1N* 10,4.
 110 B. Dent, *My Only Friend*, 32.
 111 *C* 20-21,2.
 112 *C* 35,5.
 113 *Sayings* 137.
 114 *2A* 4,2.
 115 R. Collings, *John of the Cross*, 90.
 116 *Sayings* 88.
 117 *Sayings* 26.
 118 *Ibid.* 506.
 119 P. Bourne, *St John of the Cross*, 155.
 120 *Sayings* 19.
 121 *3A* ,6,3.
 122 *C* 16,1-10.
 123 *C* 17,1-9.
 124 *C* 18,3-8.
 125 *C* 22,3.
 126 *C* 22,1.
 127 H. McCabe, O.P., *The Teaching of the Catholic Church*, p. 15.
 128 J.L. Meis, *The Experience of Nothingness in the Mystical Theology of St John of the Cross*, Doc. Thes., Berkeley: University Microfilm International, 1977, 113.
 129 *1A* 6,4.
 130 *2A* 5,7; *2N* 20,5; *C* 22,3; 24,5; 36,5; 39,5-6; *LF* 2,34; 3,78-78.
 131 'Dark Night', stanza 4.
 132 *1A* 2,1.
 133 *1A* 1,2.
 134 *Letter* 16.
 135 *2N* 25,3.
 136 *1A* 4,1-5.
 137 *LF* 1,20.
 138 *1A* 13,11.
 139 *1A* 13,13.

140　*C* 20-21,15.
141　*C* 20-21,15.
142　*3A* 20,4.
143　*3A* 23,1
144　*3A* 20,2.
145　*2A* 7,3-11.
146　*1A* 13,4.
147　*1A* 13,3-4.
148　*2A* 29,9.
149　W. Johnston, *The Mystical Way*, 321.
150　*1A* 13,3; *2A* 7,9; *2A* 29,9.
151　*2A* 7,8-9.
152　H.U. von Balthasar, *Christian Meditation* (tr., M.T. Skerry), (San Francisco: Ignatius Press, 1989), 70-71.
153　It is true that in John's major works there are only four references to Mary. But this does not diminish her value as a role-model in his writings. For him, Mary is the living embodiment of all that he has come to know and experience about union with God.
154　*C* 3,8; 20-21,11.
155　O. Rodriguez, *Saint John of the Cross*, 111-115.
156　*3A* 2,10.
157　*LF* 3,12.
158　B. Rueda, *Obedience*, 29-30.
159　H.U. von Balthasar, *Prayer* (tr., Graham Harrison), (San Francisco: Ignatius Press, 1986), 29.
160　*C* 2,8.
161　*C* 20,10.
162　D.J. Billy, *Evangelical Kernels* (New York: Alba House, 1993), 210.
163　*Lumen Gentium*, 58.
164　*Letter* 19, *The Collected Works of St John of the Cross* (tr., K. Kavanaugh and O. Rodriguez), 699.

GENERAL CONCLUSION

This book has attempted to explore the *nada* spirituality of John of the Cross, a treasure that has remained comparatively well-hidden in the field of Christianity for centuries. I hope to have demonstrated that John's *nada* spirituality is a vital piece of Christian theology and life, that offers a challenge to present and future generations. John proposed a way of *nada* well-rooted in Christian tradition, and followed the way he had proposed exactly: in doing so he transcended cultural, temporal and even religious barriers. Thus, John and his vision are admired and accepted as the common property of the whole of humanity. Though I have not had time to explore this topic in depth, I believe that his *nada* offers to the Christian Church a great opportunity to enter into a profound dialogue with other religions. Thus, it continues the 'Areopagus ministry' of Paul (Acts 17:16-34) in our multicultural and multi-religious world.

John's commentators and interpreters can fall prey to a well-intentioned tendency to water down his harsh words, perhaps to make him more acceptable. This may be the reason why his rather austere 'Sketch of Mount Carmel', which was central to the argument of this book, has attracted less attention than it should. Perhaps this lack of attention is also due to the fact that, though John valued his own sketch very much, he did not write a commentary on it. Thus, the lack of proper explanation and the repeated appearance of *nada* along the perfect path may well have served to dampen the interest of many an enthusiastic reader, and have prevented them from giving the sketch

serious thought. Another possible reason why the sketch
has been neglected, lies in the beauty of John's poetry.
Those who are carried away by the sheer beauty of 'love-
stricken bride', and her heartrending love song, may well
have preferred to overlook the strong-willed ascetic behind
the words. John did adopt the traditional imagery of bridal
mysticism to convey his teachings, but his *nada* spirituality
can be seen bursting out time and again throughout his
writings. As we noted, he wrote not "on moral and pleasing
topics addressed to the kind of spiritual people who like to
approach God along the sweet and satisfying path. We are
presenting a substantial and solid doctrine for all those
who desire to reach this nakedness of spirit."[1]

I hope to have done justice to the mind of John. The
logic behind his teachings is simple: God is all, and an
already crowded soul cannot receive a full measure of the
divine self-gift. For the individual to possess him fully
according to their capacity, they should first empty
themselves of everything that is not God. John proposed
the *kenotic* path of *nada* to help all people reach the ultimate
goal – *el todo*. We should note, however, that the immediate
beneficiaries he had in mind were his brothers and sisters
of his own Order and those closely associated with him.
The major advantage of this is the air of intimacy and
freedom that his teachings breathe, a heartfelt directness
and authenticity. The major disadvantage is the lack of
certain details that are essential for one who comes new to
his ideas: John took for granted many such details in his
description of the path towards perfection since he was
writing for the already initiated. Thus many essential details
belonging to the initial part of the journey, that it would be
useful for the more general reader to know, are absent both
from his sketch and from his description. He omitted, for
example, a consideration of the evangelical counsels and
their importance in the path towards perfection, since he
was writing to religious who were practising these counsels.

This exploration of John's teachings has, as frequently

noted, largely been a commentary on the 'Sketch of Mount Carmel', something I have never seen attempted before. Another contribution I hope to have made is the evaluation of *nada* from various points of view, providing a panoramic vision of the deep mystery of *nada*. The law of evolution that acts upon creatures brings about only minute and gradual modifications, while substantial and massive changes occur when they are sent to the abyss of *nada*. *Nada* is not only the tomb but also the womb of creation. *Nada* stands for possibilities, new beginnings and new life. God exercises his full creative power where there is *nada*. God worked efficiently 'in the beginning' because there was only *nada*, which offered "no resistance".[2] God becomes equally effective with those who embrace *nada* in their life. I hope to have enabled the reader to appreciate something of the stunning spectrum contained within *nada*.

NOTES

1   *A* Prologue, 8.
2   *1A* 6,4.

BIBLIOGRAPHICAL NOTE

The works of John of the Cross are referred to by their individual titles; the translation used is that by K. Kavanaugh and O. Rodriguez, *The Collected Works of St John of the Cross* (Revised Edition), (Washington, D.C.: ICS Publications, 1991), with amendments where it seemed to me necessary. Another important translation is that by E. Allison Peers (Tunbridge Wells: Burns and Oates, 1935).

Anyone wishing for further reading can consult the bibliographical references in the footnotes; anyone interested in reading the original Spanish text of John's works should consult the edition of José Vincente Rodríguez and Frederico Ruiz, *Obras Completas*, Madrid, EDE 1993.